DROPSHIPPING 101

How to Change Your Life Today by Starting Your First "Quick and Easy" Online Business!

ISBN-13: 979-8669794934
ISBN-10: B08F6RYJDP

Cover design by: Frédéric GOSSET

Table Of Contents

Introduction

Thank you for choosing to read **Dropshipping 101**: *How to Change Your Life today by Starting Your First Quick and Easy Online Business!*

Who wouldn't want to quit their regular 9 to 5 job to start their own business? The very thought of being your own boss is quite tempting; however, it's not uncommon to hear about someone dreaming big, not following through, and ultimately giving up on their dreams.
Starting and managing a business is not an easy venture. However, if you're interested in giving your business a try, but you aren't ready to make a huge investment or give up on a regular paycheck, at least not yet, then this book might be exactly what you need.

To start a business, you often require huge sums of capital. A lack of capital is often the primary deterrent to why many people never get entrepreneurial ventures off the ground. However, the introduction and advancement of e-commerce technology have changed all this.

Our 21st-century-world is dominated by e-commerce in just about everything we do and experience. And because access to this and other technologies has lowered barriers to entry for so many, you no longer need unrealistic amounts of money for capital; all you need is a good idea and the motivation to make it real.

Dropshipping is exactly that one innovative and very accessible approach and tool you can use to feed your entrepreneurial spirit. Regardless of what you know, or even what you think you know about dropshipping, this book will be a key resource for concepts both new and known.

Everything you need to launch and operate a successful dropshipping business is covered in this book. Topics such as the numerous advantages it offers; the proper steps to setting up a dropshipping business; selecting the right niches, products and suppliers; using affiliate marketing; Amazon FBA; and many other useful and important areas.

If you're willing to put in the required time and effort and maintain the necessary consistency, you, too, can set up a potentially lucrative dropshipping business to generate that passive income stream you've wanted to create for yourself.

Now, if you're ready to make that dropshipping dream a reality, let's start right now!

"Take a break to reshape, modify, or sustain your vision".

Robert T. KIYOSAKI, from *"Rich Dad, Poor Dad"*

Chapter 1: About Passive Income

What is Passive Income?

The premise of passive income is to create a source of income that generates money for you, but with as little effort as possible. It's often done as an addition to another job, but with something like dropshipping, if you can make it your primary income source, you must be doing something really well.

A common misconception about earning passive income is that it takes absolutely no effort to do it. Nothing could be further from the truth. More often than not, the most successful passive income earners are very busy people, and they wouldn't hesitate to tell you as much. Earning passive income takes dedication, commitment, consistency, patience, and plenty of hard work.

There are certain routine requirements of every business that need attention on an almost daily basis. Ideally, your choice of passive income business would contain as much automation built into these processes to reduce the amount of time they take up. Inherently, that is the purpose of a business being "passive".

It gives you the freedom to step away from certain repetitive, workrelated tasks to create a self-sustaining stream of income. But before you can start earning passive income, you must set up the business, invest enough initial time and energy to create or sell a product, and then continue seeking to automate that system, thereby minimizing your physical involvement.

The great thing about passive income is that it gives you complete autonomy to leverage your time and invest as much or as little as you want.

Dropshipping is a great way to earn a passive income, but be prepared to put in the effort.

Benefits of Passive Income

Hello autonomy

If you're tired of working for or under someone else, establishing your own business is a great way to remedy your situation. A dropshipping business is a great way to have autonomy over an entire business you can call your own. Working for yourself means that you run things the way you want to run them. Decisions about things like direction, marketing and scope are yours.

Goodbye mediocrity

Some large organizations don't often encourage their employees to excel in whatever they're doing. And many employees tend not to care because they don't believe their excellence is important enough. Besides, in a huge company who's going to notice?

A dropshipping business helps you to see the relationship between excellence and results. In other words, the more you put into the business, the more money you will actually see at the end of the day. Because you're driven by your own motivations, instead of the words of a manager looking over your shoulder, your business rises past mediocrity. You can see the excellence you put into it.

Work culture

More often than not, in a full-time job you don't get to choose the environment in which you're hired to work. Regardless of whether you like your colleagues or hate them, changing your situation usually isn't an option.

When you start your own business, the culture and environment are yours to create. You get to choose where and with whom you work. You can hire others to work for you, or you can stay a solo dropshipping entrepreneur.

A happy work environment and your individual investment in your business is a recipe for success.

Tax considerations

Depending on where you live and work, income tax requirements should be a top consideration. As a business owner, rather than an employee, it might be more advantageous for you to consider the passive income dropshipping business route. For example, if you work out of a home office, in some jurisdictions, your rent or portions of your mortgage might be exempt from any number of tax requirements. Of course, it would be a good idea to hire a professional accountant to better understand how it works for your dropshipping business.

Flexibility

If earning passive income is your chosen direction, instead of a regular, full-time job, you can expect to be the master of your own schedule. You're free to work whenever you want or take a month-long vacation. You could even do both of those things at the same time. With so many systems now being automated, you don't really have to be on top of everything all the time.

The flexibility of a dropshipping business can be achieved with a laptop, smartphone and a decent internet connection. You could be sipping a Mai-Tai cocktail and making money right now!

Laid off no more

These days, job security is about as common as actual pink unicorns. Even if you've been with a company for 20 years, there's no guarantee that you won't be laid off or "right-sized" tomorrow.

When you own your business, no one can fire you but...you. As long as your business is running and is making money, you will always have a job. Say goodbye to the dreaded pink slip and hello to the adorable pink unicorn!

Love your work

It's been said by countless business thought leaders and ancient philosophers: "Do what you love and you'll never work a day in your life." Nothing could be further from the truth with a passive income stream generated by dropshipping.

If you've taken the earlier advice of finding a niche you enjoy, you'll be fully invested in your business. When you turn your passion into your work, you're a step closer to the kind of success you've always wanted.

There are various benefits of passive income, and it goes beyond financial independence. We hope you decide to head in this direction.

Chapter 2: The Mind of a Passive Income Earner

Work Ethics

You have complete autonomy when it comes to creating a stream of passive income like dropshipping. However, if you don't first understand and adopt the mentality required of you while you seek out your financial independence, you're setting yourself up for either a very difficult journey or one of failure.

Perhaps you're already in this frame of mind. Or maybe you have some work to do on yourself. Either way, keep reading if you want a better understanding of what you'll be facing and the mental workout you should prepare to have.

Mindset matters

Before starting a business, getting inside your head to understand your motivations might help you prepare for many situations. Perhaps making an actual list of motivations can help you articulate. Do you want to earn money? Are you ready to quit your job? Is becoming a decision-maker important to you?

Money is certainly important, but it shouldn't be the only reason you get into a dropshipping business. A customer-loving and value-centric work ethic, as well as a positive mindset will help you on your journey to running a passive income-generating business you love.

Competition is constant

There will always be someone competing for dominance in business. And on the rare chance you corner a market in something, chances are someone will do their hardest work trying to become better than you.

This is why you not only need to be on your guard all the time, in a sense you have to be clairvoyant--you need to know your competitors' next moves and stay ahead of those. This is a game of chess with no end in sight.

As a dropshipper you must always keep up-to-date with your niche, including the other dropshippers in that space. There's no "set it and forget it" in dropshipping!

Customer service is fundamental

Regardless of how brilliant your business idea is and how revolutionary the products you are, if you aren't catering to your customers' needs, you might as well cease all business operations.

You must always work on building trust and positive relationships with existing and prospective customers. Establishing a strong and loyal customer base at the outset will boost your credibility and authority within your niche. Providing quality service to your customers should be one of your most important business goals.

Practice makes money

If you're expecting to become an overnight success as a dropshipper, you're going in the wrong direction. It takes quite a bit of work and dedication to build something up to the point where you can just sit back and count your money.

As with any endeavor, it takes practice and the chance of failure to become successful. It's okay to make mistakes--it's a great way to learn.

Prepare to put in the effort and be disciplined enough to create a business that generates a decent passive income. If you lack the drive and motivation to stick to it, you might as well keep working for someone else.

Financial responsibility

As a single business owner, there is no one else to share financial burdens. And on the more encouraging side of that coin, every bit of profit you earn is yours. You must be prepared to make sound financial decisions and take calculated risks while assuming financial responsibilities that come with starting a new business.

It's always a good idea to prepare yourself for financial difficulties, but if you spend all your time calculating and not doing, you risk missing your opportunity to become successful.

Accountable to who?

When you decide to start your own business, your only accountability is to yourself. No one else is regulating your work schedule or performance on any given day. A day of procrastination could be the cause of lost profits.

You are your own boss. Create small, measurable, achievable, realistic, and time-bound goals for yourself and the business. These goals will provide a sense of direction and keep you on track and in focus.

Forget about shortcuts

There's a difference between looking for the easy way (shortcuts) to do something and building systems in a business to ensure things run smoothly. This is true with a dropshipping business, especially because of how much it depends on automating systems. But rest assured, these are not the same as finding a way to cut corners.

If you see a self-proclaimed expert telling you how easy it is to make quick money, run the other way. Unless they're recruiting you to rob a bank or they know something about next week's lottery numbers, they're feeding you myths.

There's no shortcut to success. Be prepared to work.

Be objective

Emotions are wonderful to have. But in a business like dropshipping, you might consider leaving them out. Staying objective within your business will ensure you always make rational and informed decisions based on solid data and hard facts.

You can (and should) "trust your gut" every so often, but your business practices and decisions should be based on evidence and intelligence. You can definitely feel passionate about what you're doing, but it should not be the reason why you make a decision.

Ask for help

Everyone could use a little help. There's no shame in asking for it if you need it, especially when it comes to doing something you're not experienced in, such as accounting or marketing.

If you feel like you're going wrong somewhere, talk to others in the dropshipping world. It's always good to get a fresh perspective - or BE the fresh perspective - in any given situation.

Know when to stop

A successful business person knows when to stop. If something isn't working, move on. Stop trying to salvage the unsalvageable. If a plan isn't working, then change tactics to see what works for you. Learn to cut your losses before things get worse.

Chapter 3: Dropshipping 101

What is Dropshipping?

In your past, if you've ever looked for unique ways to earn passive income, you've likely come across the term dropshipping. It's also likely you skipped over it because you had no idea what it was or what it meant. That's okay because we're about to change that for you. If you're stepping into the world of e-commerce as a beginner, dropshipping might seem a little intimidating. Rest assured, it's a fairly straightforward concept that you'll soon understand.

Dropshipping is a simple product sales-based business model that operates without the expense and challenges of maintaining inventory. Yes, you read that correctly - no inventory means the business runs without a warehouse or, in many cases, the need for an inhouse or complicated shipping and fulfillment process.

Often considered retail sales, the dropshipper (you) sources and pairs with a dropship supplier or manufacturer of the products you want to sell. Those same suppliers or manufacturers also handle every aspect of the shipping and fulfillment process, including packaging, packing, and delivery to the dropshipper's customers (you).

Check out this (somewhat oversimplified) breakdown of the dropshipping process (in order of occurrence):

1. A customer places an order, via e-commerce, for a product listed on the dropshipper's (your) website.

2. The dropshipper (you) forwards that order to the dropship supplier or manufacturer.

3. Upon receiving the order (and payment, of course), the supplier or manufacturer packs and ships the product directly to the dropshipper's (your) customer.

That's all there is to it as a dropshipper, you're likely working in your sleep, which is the epitome of what it means to earn passive income!

The dropshipping model in 3-step process:

Benefits of Dropshipping

Now that you understand, among other things, that you can run a dropshipping business in your pajamas, let's take a more detailed look at some other advantages it offers.

Uncomplicated

If you're learning about e-commerce for the first time, setting up a dropshipping business is actually quite easy. They actually make ideal business system partners.

Another way dropshipping keeps things simple is by eliminating the need for upfront capital, physical space for a storefront and inventory warehousing (or actual inventory). It's a very simple and cost-effective way to run a business. All the cash you save can be put towards acquiring more customers!

Affordable and accessible

As a dropshipper, you're "hands-off" in areas such as purchasing or inventory warehousing. This, in turn, keeps your business expenses very low. All you really need is a place to use an internet-connected computer, a reliable internet connection, and your smartphone. There are potential added future costs to consider as your business grows. But until then, dropshipping expenses are really quite low and manageable.

Location-free

Without the need to operate from a brick and mortar location, you can work almost anywhere in the world. Dropshipping is a brilliant business model if you're a travel lover. You would need to "stay on the grid" every so often to maintain communication with suppliers and customers. Otherwise, it's lots of sales and happy trails!

Product selection

Your dropshipping business' product selection can be as varied as you want it to be (not generally recommended), or you can work with a focused niche selection (usually recommended). We'll explain this dropshipping sales

strategy in more detail further in the book. In the meantime, the rule of thumb among the dropshipping community is to start slow by selling up to five different products. Remember, you will need to coordinate your suppliers. That's why it's best to take it easy at first.

Scalability

In the conventional world of business, scalability is an often-discussed and debated concept that essentially asks how well a business might perform while undergoing operational growth and expansion (Kenton, 2019). In a non-dropshipping business, this usually means more work for all employees.

Conversely, a dropshipping business is very simple to scale. Most of the work is done by your suppliers, leaving you with some simple operational demands and taking care of your customers. While these needs can increase as you scale your dropshipping business, it hardly compares to the increasing volume of work you'd experience in a corporate job.

But Wait! The Risks!

Yes, there are risks in a dropshipping business. Do not quit your day job...yet. It does seem tempting, and it would be understandable after reading about the advantages of dropshipping. But, we don't recommend writing your resignation letter, you must also know the potential risks.

Lower profit margins

Dropshipping is quite a competitive market these days. Because the initial investment is minimal, margins are quite low when compared to regular businesses. Since it's easy to set up and the overhead is minimal, the number of people in the business is quite high. Apart from this, sellers are willing to sell their wares at lower prices to help generate more income. However, you can quickly mitigate this risk by selecting the right niche for your business. Once you're in the right niche and are selling high-quality products, you can overcome this obstacle.

No inventory

That heading is not an error. It's true--taking the inventory warehousing out of the equation is a huge advantage in a dropshipping business, but it can also be just as frustrating and risky. Your dropshipping business is entirely reliant on the inventories of thirdparty suppliers and manufacturers, many of whom are overseas. There are too many potential situations, over which you have zero control, that could negatively affect your product supplies - factory fires, union strikes, defective parts, and more. There are ways to mitigate these risks, and they are most definitely included further on.

Shipping charges

As a dropshipper, you must be prepared to work with multiple suppliers at once. Most of the products you list on your website will be sourced through various suppliers or manufacturers located across the globe. We'll get into this a bit further down. But suffice it to say, this can make the shipping process and pricing a little tricky. For example, if one customer ordered four products from four different suppliers, the dropshipper will incur different shipping charges on each of these products. To overcome this obstacle, spend time crunching some numbers with the intention of making it affordable to include these charges in the retail cost of the product.

It's always your fault

If something goes wrong with a dropshipping order over which you had no control, and your customer is affected, it will always be your fault. If there was a devastating typhoon in the country of your supplier, and it destroyed the factory or warehouse, and everything inside of it including your customer's order, it will be your fault. Something like that will happen to you, as it's happened to even the most experienced dropshippers.

Your only course of action is to correct the "not your fault but still your fault" error. It's your business, your customer is unhappy. Your goal, to the best of your ability, is to turn their frown upside down.

If you've read this far, and intend to continue, that's a great sign! If you think the advantages of a dropshipping business far outweigh the risks, you've officially done your dropshipping due diligence and you're ready to continue. Excellent! Keep reading! Things get way more interesting from here on out.

Creating a Dropshipping Business

Now that you're aware of the different benefits of dropshipping, it's time to dive a little deeper - not too deep just yet - by learning about the six basic steps every first-time dropshipper must follow to get their business started the correct way.

Step 1: Pick the right niche

Identifying the best niche for your dropshipping business is possibly one of the most important requirements when launching your business. This is because your identified niche is going to help you pick which products to sell. Essentially, you're zeroing in on your target customer demographic.

For example, if you've determined your niche market (your customer demographics) to be comfortable footwear for executive-level career women, this would, in turn, establish the criteria for the type of shoes you should be selling; namely, shoes that female executives would want.

A niche can be any number of different criteria. Another good example could be teen boys in lower-income neighborhoods who love science fiction. Your dropshipping product line could be affordable licensed clothing and other collectibles related to popular movies in that genre.

More importantly, your chosen niche should be something enjoyable for you. If you aren't passionate about it, how are you going to create convincing marketing to build your customer base? That's the beauty of a dropshipping business - you can choose to be passionate about your work rather than simply going through the motions every day simply to pay the bills. Why choose to do something like this if you're going to lose interest?

Here are some other considerations for when you're ready to figure out your niche:

Profit Potential

What can you sell? What do you want to sell? If you're concerned about whether or not you should focus on selling expensive or inexpensive products, ideally within a niche you've chosen, your efforts will usually be in marketing and customer acquisition. It's really quite simple - without customers, you sell nothing. No sales mean no money. So if you're stuck trying to decide if your marketing efforts should be to sell an exclusive, $1,500 "timepiece" or a practical $20 wristwatch, err on the side of products with the greatest profit potential for you.

Shipping Costs

Typically, the dropshipping business will have very little control over determining a supplier's shipping logistics and costs to get products to customers. That is usually the domain of the supplier or manufacturer. However, as the owner of the dropshipping business, you do have control over whether or not to sell a product with high shipping costs. If that one thing is preventing you from selling your product, you can stop selling that product. It might be helpful to reexamine your chosen niche to understand the shipping needs and why it may or may not cost so much. Most importantly, stick to niches that favor low cost or free shipping. Regardless, the supplier has likely already factored it into the price of the product.

Find Your Customers Easily

For customer acquisition and product planning, Google is a dropshipper's absolute BFF. You can use its trend and/or keyword planner tools as your digital gut-checker. Both tools can help you determine if people are actually looking for or even talking about your chosen niche and related products. However, this works best only if your aim is to enter a smaller market. If this is what you're doing, you're probably aiming to supply something that people are having trouble finding. Otherwise, you can take advantage of trends and sell items that people search for more often. The latter is easier and will allow you to take advantage of the high demand for a product while it's trending.

Impulse Shoppers

Not everyone gets online with the intention of buying. Most users often scroll through different websites before they actually make their purchases. Therefore, as a dropshipper, your target audience must include impulsive buyers. Not just impulsive buyers, but those individuals who have sufficient disposable income to afford the products you're selling.

Your primary focus must be to drive traffic to your business website so that you have an extremely high rate of conversion since most of these visitors might not return. The products you're selling must appeal to impulsive buyers and must be priced such that the buyers will be tempted to make a purchase immediately. Some tactics to encourage impulse buying include selecting the right products for the targeted customers, correct product placement and grabbing their attention visually by using bright colors or banners.

White Label Products

A great thing about the dropshipping business is that you can build a business brand by selling products created from ideas of already successful products. Provided there aren't any copyright or intellectual property rights issues, these "white label" products can be sold under your own label or brand name. If it was a good idea for one segment of the population, it may also succeed within the one you're targeting for your own business. One thing to remember when you're looking for white label products is to make sure the packaging is legitimate as well. You wouldn't want to sell your own branded product inside of a faked well-known brand.

Foreign Ain't Borin'

This is an oversimplified analogy - if you've decided you want to build a dropshipping business to sell oranges, you won't make a dent in the state of Florida. If your customers can take a walk and buy your product down the street from them, you might reconsider your niche or your target customers. Sell products that aren't easily bought where they live or adjust your demographics.

You can see now why niche selection is so important. If you've got yours figured out, that's great. It may work for a while or you may need to adjust your parameters in the end. Regardless of where you land in this particular process, remember, there are still five more steps to go!

Step 2: Understand the competition...or lack thereof

So, you've chosen a niche. Congratulations!

Step 1? Check!

And now you've got your eye on a product to sell. It's SO incredibly unique, no one else is selling it! Come on! That's amazing! No competition...

Whoa, friend! Full stop, please! Let's give this a bit more consideration, okay? "There's no competition!" could be the discovery of a lifetime, or it could be the Titanic of dropshipping products.

For now, let's go with this: "Huh! Well, that sounds way too good to be true!" So, here are five reasons why you should probably find out if it is...too good to be true:

1. The product is so new, the supplier is calling you "My little Guinea Pig". Do you take your chances or head for the hills?

2. The shipping rates are crazy high. It would be cheaper for you to take a luxury cruise to your supplier to retrieve the product and deliver it yourself.

3. Related to number 2, if shipping isn't an issue, but the supplier has caught on to your excitement and added a mysterious "passion tax", thereby making it nearly impossible to sell profitably, just don't. Please.

4. Of course, you could look into the supplier/manufacturer. Is it something they're doing to make the product unsalable? It could be shoddy manufacturing or something more exotic and super gross.

5. Is it actually a terrible product? Seriously. Ask a friend. Show it to your mom or cousin Elwood. Just get a second or third opinion. Maybe your non-existent competitors are trying to tell you something. Or maybe...

WARNING: BONUS FOOD FOR THOUGHT!

6. ...you are that dropshipping "out of thin air" phenom—a marketing messiah if you will, who could science-magic a cool topsy-turvy, inside out, world-peace inspiring way to make a buck from this competition-free product! But really, probably not...

To make a short story super long—but really fun to read—there's nothing wrong with competition in dropshipping. If anything, you could still have a shot at number 6.

Step 3: Finding pink unicorn makers

The first rule of finding good and reliable dropshipping suppliers is to look in your own backyard. Sourcing products locally, especially if your customers are also nearby, or at least close enough to minimize shipping and other costs.

And really, if you find one of these pink unicorn suppliers, you should also take your baby dropshipping self out to buy a jackpot lottery ticket - unless you live overseas, that rarely happens.

Until then, the rest of the supplier search might feel like you're looking for a blade of grass in a field...of grass. And yet, contrary to all of our screaming 21st-century instincts, you might assume that heading over to everybody's most reliable search engine, Google, would be the first place to start. It could be. But, it's not.

But, if you're the type of person who needs to touch fire to know if it's really all that hot, so to speak, start with Google (Scary!); but do yourself a favor and instead of searching for the actual product (like "pink unicorn phone cases"), do yourself a favor and do a search for "dropship suppliers".

When Googling is out of your system, put your sweaty hands back on your laptop, open a brand new browser window and check out Aliexpress.com. Largely considered one the first easy-to-navigate dropshipping platform, it is by no means the only one of its kind. For now, it's a great place to start.

The interesting thing about Aliexpress and other platforms out there is that they, too, can be super overwhelming, especially if you have no idea what you're looking for, or when all you want is to find a great supplier of pink unicorn tech accessories of only the highest quality. The point is, this is a process and if you don't do your due diligence, that one delivery of an electric blue unicorn case that fits the wrong smartphone could be your dropshipping downfall.

Start by making an extensive list of all suppliers and/or manufacturers of horned mythical animal-based products and conduct your own interview process for each one. We'll delve a bit deeper into many of these later on in the book, but to get you started on your due diligence, here's a basic list of what you should find out about them:

- Be on the same page about expectations from them and be as clear about what they expect from you

- Know what their response times are for different scenarios: defective product, urgencies, disputes, etc.

- Decide at the beginning if you feel the language barrier will be an issue.

- Ask about their manufacturing and fulfillment processes, if they're just a broker, a wholesaler or the manufacturer of all unicorn products in the entire Czech Republic.

- Read their other customer testimonials and/or ask other dropshippers about them.

- Definitely find out if they're able to scale their processes as you scale your business. After reading this book, we're pretty sure it will.

The best tip about finding suppliers for unicorn products and whatever else you want to sell as a dropshipper is to ask questions all the time until you're satisfied with what you're seeing.

Step 4: Get those pink unicorns online

Wow! It's only the fourth step and you already know where to look for potential dropshipping suppliers of all things pink unicorns! Now, let's look at how you're going to set up your storefront.

Remember, this is e-commerce. No bricks and no mortar. It's all online for you. The best place to start looking is a service that is best suited to support the dropshipping business model. Start your e-commerce platform search with Shopify, Magento, and OpenCart. There are others, but this is your starting place for now.

Most of these services are created to be end-user friendly. You don't really need any technical training to understand how they work, but you should do some comparison shopping before committing to one. Examine each one in terms of things like ease of use, set-up time, fee structure (yes, there are fees), different features, and levels of customer and technical support. Read others' reviews of these services as well.

You could also go the more DIY route with a website built on platforms like Wordpress or Wix, both of which have different ways to "plugin" e-commerce functionalities. And with any of these platforms, you have the option of building it yourself or hiring a professional to do it for you. For now, it's recommended you start with as much assistance as you can afford.

Step 5: Find pink unicorn customers

To review, you know what you're selling (product), to whom you're selling (demographically), how you're selling (online service), and now it's time to find some actual paying customers.

This is the stage in which you get out there to let everyone know who you are and what you're selling. Most of us just call this "sales". The simplest way to start is by using social media, with Facebook and Instagram being your first (and often the best) platforms to reach your targeted customers.

Through both of these social media platforms, you can use hypertargeted advertising campaigns to let your potential customers know about you and your products. You actually stand a fair chance at making sales and generate revenue quickly.

Apart from social media marketing, you can also use email marketing, which consists of building an email list for your business and using it to reach out directly to your potential customers.

Search engine optimization is another helpful approach and we'll get into this and everything else is later chapters.

Step 6: Get better at selling pink unicorns

Your work doesn't just stop now that you've got a dropshipping business up and running. Your need to do mundane things will certainly lessen once you automate routine tasks, but your responsibility as a business owner certainly doesn't end here.

There's always a better and more efficient way to optimize your business to reduce the time and costs incurred as you expand your scope and earn more. To do this, you need to continue tracking and analyzing metrics generated from your online marketing campaigns and your business website. This is how you can begin to understand where your business and its marketing are succeeding and where improvements are needed.

An analytical tool like Google Analytics can produce data and metrics to track the "customer journey" from start to purchase with the goal of optimizing your business and, of course, your profitability.

Common Dropshipping Mistakes

Dropshipping newbies will make mistakes when they first start out. That's why this section could be super important. It may seem like a dropshipping crystal ball, but rest assured, these are just the wellknown mistakes. There are other kinds and you will make them. In the meantime, try to avoid these, if you can.

Mistake #1: crazy shipping charges

You must know all you can about potential shipping charges. Of all the expenses in dropshipping, this one can seriously eat into your profits if you're not careful or strategic. Shipping charges change depending on the origin of the product. Your best bet is to calculate a flat shipping rate. This will make the rest of your calculations easier to do. Not to mention, it will reduce your stress and make things easier for your customers.

Mistake #2: shipping issues

There's no shortage of shipping issues that might happen with dropshipping. So, before you commit to a supplier, make sure you have a list of potential issues that could happen, as well as possible solutions to those issues. By doing this, essentially you're working on improving your customer relations while making the customer feel heard.

Mistake #3: easy money

A common mistake a lot of dropshippers make is that dropshipping means easy money. Yes, dropshipping is certainly easier than a regular job. However, it does require plenty of hard work. If you're not prepared to put in all this effort, you can forget about earning anything more than a failing business. Certainly, automation can help, but it shouldn't replace your dedication and effort to grow the business.

Mistake #4: relying on single suppliers

Relying on a single supplier of a product is a recipe for disaster. What do you do if that supplier goes out of business or something happens to their factory? You must always have more than one supplier of a particular product. Another important tip about suppliers is to have a legal contract between you. It can help mitigate any potential conflicts should something happen.

Mistake #5: forgettable branding

Ensuring your customers remember you for their next purchases (or even their first) is practically its own job. Keep your business name and logos as top-of-mind as possible by displaying it as often as possible throughout their purchasing journey. That happens on your website.

You can do the same by adding your information to custom packing slips and a product's actual packaging. Another great idea to stay topof-mind is to remain engaged with your customers. Sending personal emails after purchase is a great way to set yourself apart from the other businesses who don't care as much about customers as you do.

Mistake #6: poor customer communication

If you promise your customers a hassle-free and fast shipping turnaround, then you need to stick to it. All the information you provide about their order status must be easy to understand and easily accessible. If the customer can't find this information, you risk losing them as a loyal and repeat customer. Not only that, but you also risk your customers telling others about their bad experience. You don't have to be on Yelp for too long to know what a bad review looks like.

Mistake #7: changes and cancellations

It never fails: a customer will almost always order something "by accident" or make some other mistake. That's okay. Humans make mistakes. As the responsible dropshipper, it's up to you to ensure you can help them fix their mistakes. Be ready to cancel an order. Make sure you can change the order.

Just make sure your customer is happy enough to continue buying your products.

Mistake #8: return complications

Communicate your return policies as often and as prominently as possible. There might be different reasons why a customer might want to return an order. You must have a return policy in place. It must not only include guidelines associated with the return of the product but the refunds as well.

Chapter 4: Products and Suppliers

Finding the Best Products

Now that you're better acquainted with the world of dropshipping, it's time to really get down to business. As mentioned above, one of the most important steps in starting a dropshipping business is product research. The products you choose to sell form the backbone of a successful dropshipping business.

While selecting a product, there are three important criteria to keep in mind:

- Profitability
- Demand
- Fulfillment

When a product meets all three of these, you have a winner. So, it's obvious that product research is a vital requirement of any dropshipping business. Keep in mind that product research is not easy. You'll need to sift through various e-commerce platforms and perform online research to come up with the best suitable products for your dropshipping business.

Once you have a list of potential products, you then need to study the trends related to that product in your niche. You also need to know who the competitors are and calculate how to turn a profit.

Here are some of the ways you can get started with product research:

Start thinking

The importance of taking the time to brainstorm your product selection strategies is often lost on many new dropshippers.

While selecting products for your business, you must know if the selected product is conducive to being sold online. One way to approach this list is to think about the things people use on a daily basis and find products that can help make those things easier and faster. Everyone wants more time in their day. Start with that.

Before you select a specific product, spend the necessary time required to analyze the different options available to you carefully. At first glance, an idea might seem ridiculous but don't brush it off too soon.

Social shopping

Virtual marketplaces, also known as social shopping websites, such as Wish.com or Etsy.com, have become quite popular lately. These online marketplaces contain user-tested products that are often promoted by "influencers" in a particular niche.

By searching through different social shopping websites, you can see the products that many online shoppers are buying. These sites also curate lists of popular products people are buying. That information is dropshipping gold!

Opinions matter

Never ignore the importance of someone else's experience. Talk to other dropshippers in your niche, and connect with them. It might provide you with valuable insight into their success. You can also take note of your competitors' websites, the images they use, and their sales tactics. Even if it doesn't give you any immediate ideas, you might find some other inspirations for your own business.

Pricing strategy

Pricing your products to maximize profits, while remaining affordable for your customers, is a key to successful sales. But instead of arbitrarily setting a price, you need to know how much you, as the retailer, have to pay for the product and the maximum you can charge the customer.

The retail price is the maximum price at which a product can be sold. An ideal product for dropshipping can retail for anywhere between $15 to $200. Even if the margin between these two numbers seems rather large, amongst other dropshippers, that's what is considered the sweet spot for finding the perfect dropshipping product.

When you start listing products that are seen as affordable by your targeted customers, it's likely your sales volume will increase. It also enables you to obtain more valuable feedback from your customers to improve your business. However, if your pricing is too low, it's far more difficult to make ends meet.

During the course of setting your prices, be mindful of any MSRPs (manufacturer's suggested retail pricing) associated with it. If there's an MSRP on a product, you can never exceed it.

However, you can always tweak your profit margins by working with the minimum advertised price or the minimum retail price of a product. For instance, certain brand manufacturers will prevent others from selling their products at a price lower than the minimum MSRP specified by them. This is perhaps one of the reasons why you don't see any Apple products being sold at a lower price than the MRP unless there's a sale going on with the actual manufacturer. If an iPhone is retailed at $700, then you cannot sell it at $600 because you want to attract more customers. Apple prohibits this expressly. So, carefully go through market policies associated with the products you wish to sell as a dropshipper.

Profit margins

A profit margin is the percentage of earnings after deducting all costs and expenses related to obtaining your product. While deciding how to price your products, you must consider profit margins. After all, if you're not earning a profit, what's the point? Profit margins on any product you sell must be between 20 and 40 percent. The more you increase your markup at the retail price, the higher your profits.

If you're selling a product that retails at $180, you can establish your profit margins anywhere between 20 to 30 percent on that product. So on that $180 product, your profit calculates to anywhere from $36 to $54. It's quite easy to establish a profit margin, especially when what you're selling is more expensive.

So, can a dropshipper earn money by selling lower-priced products? The short answer is yes. But you need to be very thorough in your research to ensure you can actually make money.

There are a few factors to keep in mind when selecting a low-priced product for your dropshipping business. They are shipping charges, marketing costs, miscellaneous expenses for branding and marketing, and packaging costs. They matter for all dropshipping product pricing, but when it comes to selling the smaller items, they become far more crucial in setting your prices to maximize profits.

Dimensions and weight

The size and weight of your product matter quite a bit in dropshipping. The best products are the easiest ones to ship to customers. A rule of thumb is to find products that can fit into a standard-sized shoe box. Anything larger will wreak havoc on your shipping and packaging expenses and eat into your own profits. Some shipping partners might specify the maximum and minimum weight requirements for the products they ship. So, before committing to a supplier, understand what their shipping charges and policies are for different sized products.

Durability

Related to the previous tip about dimensions and weight, you should do yourself a huge favor right now and vow never to sell products that are delicate, fragile or very breakable. The few moving parts a product has is also recommended. Even if there are a niche market and a gigantic demand for porcelain miniature pink unicorns, you have no guarantee they'll be handled with the care you might expect. And then while your fragile pink unicorns are in transit, even the slightest jarring movements could cause cracks or breaks. If you're just getting started in dropshipping, stick to products that can survive bumpy shipping journeys.

Consider the turnover

Sometimes, a product gets discontinued for any number of reasons. Perhaps they've been updated to a newer version, or a specific feature or color is no longer offered by the manufacturer. This matters to you for various reasons. You could end up spending considerable time and resources on marketing, advertising, branding, and packaging only to realize the product isn't available. The products with more seasonality built into them require much updating with things like content or photos. To reduce these costs, it's better to find products with lower chances of turnover.

Trial and error

Once you've finalized your list of viable products for your dropshipping business, it's recommended that you actually test them yourself. Why does product testing matter? Quite simply, if it doesn't work well or the quality is terrible, you won't want to sell it. Even if a product looks perfect on paper, the reality might be very different. It also shows you what it's like to work with a particular supplier/manufacturer. Most suppliers are willing to send you free samples if they feel you're a genuine potential customer. You may have to pay a small fee to get these samples from some suppliers but the small expense is worth it in the long run.

Repeat business through subscriptions

One of the best ways of finding the best product is sticking to a product you chose and liked before. If you offer good quality products, fair pricing, and stellar customer service, your customers are bound to continue buying from you. However, a new trend has gained a fair bit of traction among consumers - product subscription services. A variety of products, ranging from clothing, cosmetics, chocolate, or even personal hygiene, are sold as subscriptions whereby the customer pays to receive a regularly delivered product within a fixed time period (weekly, monthly, quarterly, etc.)

As a dropshipping seller, you stand to create a really nice and steady stream of income through subscription offerings. Impulse buyers are great to have, but to have some stability a subscription service is basically a loyal customer who wants to continue buying your products.

Some of the best products to choose for this type of offering include healthcare products, personal hygiene, cosmetics, fashion items, or anything else used daily.

Common Product Mistakes

When you're learning, you will end up making a few mistakes. It's not only common, but it's a part of the learning process. In this section, you'll learn about the most common mistake Newby dropshippers tend to make while selecting products for the business. Carefully go through the information and come up with a plan that will help you avoid these common mistakes.

Mistake #1: selling big brands and designer products

Avoid these products at all costs. While the prospect of selling big brand and designer products is rather tempting, there are a few issues here. The rules surrounding what you can sell and how much you can make from them are heavily dictated by the companies and suppliers. There's very little wiggle room for strategic pricing. This keeps the profit margins very low. Unless you have deep pockets for the real brands, you'd be wise to stay away from them altogether. Stick to safer private-label or generic products.

Mistake #2: counterfeit, knockoffs, replicas, first copies

Selling knockoffs or anything else presented as officially branded might seem tempting. But is that really a risky path you want to take? Despite the demand for these products, it's never worth the risk. Copyright infringement issues, trademark violations, and other intellectual property rights issues are quite common. Usually, if a supplier or manufacturer is selling very big name labels for well under what they normally sell for, just move on. In other words, if it's too good to be true, it's a knockoff.

Mistake #3: too much competition

If your chosen niche seems to have lots of competition, while it obviously means there's plenty of demand for those products, it also could be that much more difficult for you to sell - especially if you're new to dropshipping. For example, if the product you choose to sell is trending and considered "hot" or "in", you aren't the first person to jump on the opportunity. You're better off starting with a product that has moderate demand, at least until you get a foothold in the dropshipping business.

Finding the Best Suppliers

While deciding on the niche and products you wanted to sell, were you able to take note of the suppliers/manufacturers? If you were unsure about whether or not they were worth using, this section will help with those questions.

The success of your dropshipping business is dependent on several factors. But really, if you don't have the right suppliers/manufacturers, you don't have a business. All your time and effort spent on finding ideal products, creating a professional website, and promoting it are useless without suppliers. Since the stakes are so high, it's important that you spend a lot of time finding and vetting suppliers before you commit to any of them.

You should also understand the difference between suppliers and manufacturers. Manufacturers actually produce the items you're selling. You can contact manufacturers directly to get their products at a lower cost. A supplier adds its own price to the manufacturing cost when they sell to you. You may not always have the option to deal directly with a manufacturer for many products. One reason for this is that manufacturers prefer selling their products in bulk instead of single items. Nonetheless, contacting manufacturers to find out the actual price of products will also help you to haggle a better price with any supplier you're considering.

There are two scenarios for when you might start looking for a supplier. The first scenario is when you have a specific product in mind. In the second scenario, you need to have a product or a supplier. Let's take a look in detail at both these scenarios. Since you're just getting started with dropshipping, it's a good idea to start looking for a product as well as a supplier for that product simultaneously. It reduces your workload and makes research easier.

Decide the product first

If you've narrowed down the product you want to sell, it's time to find a supplier. As a dropshipper, you rely on your supplier completely to fulfill your incoming orders. You'll find a few suppliers who are not only reliable but also have the best quality products on-hand to ship to your customers quickly. These are top-tier suppliers, anything below this level of quality will negatively impact your business.

Research your competition

Once you make a list of potential suppliers, you can further narrow it down by figuring out where your competitors source their products. It's quite easy to identify top-performing brands and products on ecommerce platforms-- they're not only listed on the homepages of the platforms themselves, but they also have a considerable social media presence. While checking different marketplaces like Amazon, go through the "Popular Products" category.

In this stage, make a list of all your competitors, as well as the products they sell. Also, note the product suppliers. Go through these two steps for all competitors within your niche. It not only gives you insight into the products that are selling well but also the reasons why your competitors are doing well.

Not too many top tier sellers are great at marketing. So, finding them isn't going to be that easy. Be prepared for plenty of legwork for this stage.

Contact suppliers

Once you've made a list of suppliers, contact them. Talk to them about their policies and determine whether or not they meet your requirements. Start narrowing down the list of suppliers and then order samples from them. If any of your competitors are using a supplier you're considering, order a product from your competition. It will give you a better idea of how the supplier operates.

While researching suppliers, consider the different physical stores you can visit to buy the items you want to sell. If these brick and mortar stores haven't stepped into the world of online selling, it might make for a good supplier. If you think this is a viable option, ask the business they'd like to sell their products online for a commission. If the business you approach doesn't have any online presence, you might have to explain dropshipping and your business proposal to them.

Service aggregators

Aggregators provide a list of dropship suppliers for a fee. These aggregators are well aware that most dropshippers struggle to find top tier suppliers in a niche. However, aggregators tend to attract many new dropshippers who are looking for shortcuts to success. Most toptier suppliers prefer not to associate themselves with aggregators or any other similar service providers. When you reach out to a leading supplier without the use of an aggregator, it demonstrates your interest, seriousness, and commitment to doing what's best for your business.

Evaluate suppliers

Now that you have a list of suppliers, there are different factors you must consider when making your selections. Don't be in a rush to commit to any suppliers until you've done as much due diligence as possible. After all, profitability, as well as the credibility of your dropshipping business, largely depends on the suppliers you choose.

Let's look at some factors to consider throughout your selection process.

MAP policies

MAP refers to a supplier's "minimum advertised price" policies, which are a set of guidelines created to protect their business interests. In other words, it's the lowest price at which the supplier's products can be sold by a retailer. Top tier suppliers will always enforce their MAP policies quite effectively. It also helps minimize arbitrary pricing and price wars among dropshippers and other retailers. This is why it's better to select suppliers with rigid MAP policy enforcement.

The simplest way to check this is by going through the multiple listings of the product on Google Shopping and finding the lowest common price for that specific product. For example, if the lowest listed price for a product is $20, and if no other business is selling it at a lower price, this is an indicator that the supplier enforces its MAP policies. Usually, from the perspective of a dropshipper, this value represents the lowest profit margin chargeable for a product. If you think the profit margin is too low, you might need to reconsider your product choice.

Fees to sell

Some suppliers charge a monthly or annual fee simply to sell their products. These suppliers are not considered top tier. Rather, it's indicative of a supplier that is more interested in making quick money instead of building a sustainable brand. A top tier supplier not only understands the value of a dropshipping business it also understands the opportunities it presents. If you find a supplier using a pay-to-play policy, run the other way.

Punctuality

If a supplier cannot fulfill orders on time, it can affect your business' credibility. Find a supplier who is as invested in the business as you are. If their attitude toward delivery timing and shipping policies is too carefree, you will certainly run into some trouble. Regardless of how brilliant the product, if they're not delivered on time, your business will suffer.

Proximity

Your chosen suppliers don't have to be right next door to you, but the closer they are, the better it is for your business. Close suppliers allow you to better scrutinize their service policies and gives you a better opportunity to get to know them.

Before finalizing your supplier list, double-check to ensure they don't supply to your competitors and review the signed contract to make sure all correct terms and conditions are clearly outlined. We'll look at these in later sections of this book.

Chapter 5: Getting to "Yes" with Suppliers

Now that you've found a top-tier supplier for your business, the next step is to connect and negotiate with suppliers for the best deal and to agree on the terms of that deal. In this section, you will learn about how to get from communicating to negotiating to questioning, and finally, to signing with suppliers.

Learn to Negotiate

This section is all about the different negotiation tactics you can employ while dealing with potential suppliers to help get you the best possible deal for your business.

Prioritize your business

The profitability of your business must be your number one priority, which is why it's important to know how to negotiate with potential suppliers. You have to be cautious about this because negotiating can be a little tricky with suppliers. You can promise them high monthly sales or anything else to convince them to do business with you. But, even if you make these lofty claims, as a new dropshipper, you're missing the proof to back them up.

A dropshipper supplier in this scenario will just have to take your word for it. When you look at it from the perspective of the supplier, you're a newbie with no experience. So, be prepared to deliver an excellent sales pitch, by making it as appealing and convincing as possible. If you can't deliver on any of your claims, don't make any. This is the only way you can gain the supplier's trust, especially if you're only intending on paying them after the product is sold.

Legal business = legitimate business

While dropshipping is considered a legal business, you still have to be careful about who you do business with. There are many dropshippers who've had negative experiences with untrustworthy suppliers.

A potential supplier should be able to produce the relevant documentation to you. Check that the supplier is running a legitimate business, with proof of registration on URL registries, government documents, or other official documentation. This way you have a better chance at establishing a trustworthy relationship from the outset. Suppliers will usually check up on you before they do business with you, but that should go both ways.

Have a contract

With any supplier, you need a contract outlining the terms and conditions for the relationship. Look for clauses describing the provision of services, penalties for services not provided, and remedies for any breach of contract by either of the parties. Make sure you and the supplier are on the same page regarding communication, payment terms, and other contractual requirements.

How you communicate with a supplier also should be clear prior to entering into a contract. Include details about how information is to be shared, how they confirm receipt of orders, and anything related to delivery. You can always hire a lawyer with experience in this area to help you navigate the process.

Order fulfillment

This is one of the most important aspects of a dropshipping business-the payable commissions after order fulfillment. You will receive a commission, which will be the percentage of every sale you've made. The commission percentage must be about 15% for normal products and 25 to 30 percent for any low-priced items. Apart from this, you decide on the payment method. The questions you must answer are:

- What is the commission rate?
- When are commissions paid?
- How are commissions paid?
- How often per month are commissions paid?

Ideally, pay the supplier only after the sale; namely, after you're paid by the customer. Never pay any sum to the supplier before the expiration of the period of return. For example, if you already paid the supplier and the customer decides to return the product, this will exacerbate your issues and create more problems. Also, consider exchange rates when dealing with international suppliers.

While drawing up a contract of work with the supplier, make sure that you include clauses related to warranties, guarantees, and returns. Clearly specify what will happen and the course of action when a customer returns an order. Remember to mention who will bear the expenses and the procedures associated with the product replacement.

In a dropshipping business, you must ensure products or orders are delivered to the customer within the specified time. So, include a related clause in the contract. The supplier must comply with the deadlines and must ship the product according to the terms stated in the contract. Include the mode of delivery, the delivery partners related, and the time for order fulfillment. Once the contract is drafted and all changes are made, make sure that you and the supplier agree to all terms.

Once you've reached an agreement, check whether or not the compensation provided is sufficient. After all this, it's time to sign the contract. Once the contract is signed, it's legally binding for both parties.

If things don't progress the way you planned or if you run into any trouble because of the supplier, it's time to cut your losses and move on. Revisit your list of suppliers and find someone else. This is one of the reasons why you must work with more than one supplier. Even if one of them backs away, you can rely on the others.

Questions to Ask Suppliers

What are their payment terms?

Do they expect payment immediately or can you negotiate termed payment plans, like upon customer receipt of the product, or after a certain pre-negotiated timeframe, like 30 days?

Are there hidden or extra fees?

Ask suppliers if they charge extra fees related to delivery, fuel surcharges, returns, or even duties on any imported products.

Do they sell direct to consumers?

Does the supplier sell the same products as retail, or directly to customers. If so, that supplier has just become a competitor.

Will they meet your price?

The selling price of a product minus its cost will give you the gross margin on a specific product. This is your profit after completion of the sale. Even if you're setting the price of the product, a top tier supplier will help you understand what the other sellers are charging for the same product.

What is their return policy?

When a customer wants to return a product, you must be fully aware of how the supplier deals with these situations.

What is their warranty policy for defective products?

If a product malfunctions or is below quality, it's important to understand if a supplier offers warranties on their products and what their terms involve.

How often do they increase prices?

Suppliers also need to focus on their profit margins. So, it would make little sense for them to raise prices and risk losing customers to their competitors. It could happen, so it can't hurt to ask.

Who is your regular point of contact?

Do you deal with a third party representative or are you communicating directly with the supplier? Or are both options available? In addition to this, if time zones are an issue, is someone always available to speak during your local business hours?

Will you be informed of new product offerings?

As a dropshipper, you need to stay current by offering new products. Ask your suppliers if they'll give you advanced notice of any new products coming available.

Dropshipping Scams to Avoid

The most trusted and credible supplier directories are SaleHoo, Dropship Direct, and Worldwide Brands. Sourcing suppliers using these lists is the best way to minimize any potential scamming. Regardless of where you find your suppliers, here are some of the common red flags to note:

Red Flag #1: charging monthly fees

If a supplier charges monthly fees, they're in it to scam you. Do not pay membership fees to any suppliers.

Red Flag #2: payment restrictions

A supplier should be open to accepting credit cards or direct payments. A payment is legitimate no matter how it's made. A good supplier should know this.

Red Flag #3: not displaying badges

A good supplier should display all of their business-related badges, such as the Better Business Bureau (BBB), or others that might convey their trustworthiness as a business.

Red Flag #4: new domain names

Use any number of online domain registries to find out when a supplier registered their domain. If it's less than a year old, they could be a risky partnership. You can also do a Google search of the supplier's name and the word "scam" to see what comes up. This is a great way to find any bad reviews on that supplier.

Red Flag #5: no known address or telephone

Look up the address of the supplier and then call them. This is perhaps the simplest way to spot a fraudulent supplier. If they don't answer the phone or when they do, they can't answer your questions directly, you should think twice before using them for your business.

Red Flag #6: poor service from the start

If a supplier wants your business, they'll deliver orders on time and as promised. If they can't do that from day one, it's a sure sign of future challenges.

Chapter 6: **Sales Platforms**

Now that you're aware of what dropshipping means, it's time to learn more about how to start a dropshipping business. Once you have a good product idea in mind and are aware of the suppliers you can use, it brings us to the next step in the process -- finding a sales platform.

Popular dropshipping suppliers include AliExpress, Megagoods, Alibaba, and Wholesale Central, to name a few. Different dropshipping services you can use include Doba, SaleHoo, Oberlo, Wholesale2b, Dropship Direct, and more.

An e-commerce platform enables you to easily build your own online storefront without having to do so yourself. E-commerce platforms provide all the required tools, making it easier to set up and manage your store.

Selecting a good e-commerce platform is the next step in setting up a dropshipping business. Plenty of people opt for Amazon or eBay, but there are several other options available as well. When it comes to picking the right platform, you must look at the features it includes and how they can help your business. Let's look at the different options available, including some of their features.

WooCommerce

One of the most popular e-commerce platforms, if you wish to create a store that offers basic functionality with ease-of-use, WooCommerce is perfect for you. When compared to the other e-commerce platforms in this section, WooCommerce is best for beginners. From the perspective of a developer, this platform is a little tricky to customize; and most of its extended functionality must be acquired using thirdparty plugins.

Features

This platform is equipped with fundamental features like product catalogs, preinstalled payment gateways, inventory management, shipping calculation, various shipping methods, geolocation support, sales report, discount or coupon codes, auto taxes, and much more. Then there are several thousands of plugins available for this platform.

Time and cost

This is a free plugin to be used on a Wordpress website. So, you must first create a website on WordPress and then install the WooCommerce plugin. The time it takes to build a website on this platform is less than the other platforms. If you have no technical knowledge, you might need some help. It may cost anywhere from $1500-$3500 to build on this platform. However, the cost will increase if you require any advanced features, other plugins or customization.

Ease-of-use

The user interface offered by this platform is intuitive, simple, and easy to understand. It's quite easy even for beginners to understand. If you're just getting started with dropshipping, it's better to opt for a platform that isn't too complicated. All the features provided by WooCommerce are ideal for store managers.

Scalability and support

This platform is ideal for all small dropshipping businesses. If you wish to start a medium or a large e-commerce store, then opt for the other options discussed in this section. The performance of this platform is negatively affected when the number of products on your dropshipping site increases. When you run into a problem, you can easily find the solution by looking at the documentation or by contacting the support team. If you wish to integrate any dropshipping function to a website on this site, you're required to install a third-party plugin that costs $49 or more. This is one of the features of WooCommerce and unless you install certain plugins, you cannot make the most of the functionality offered by this platform.

Magento

Magento is an incredibly powerful e-commerce platform, which is available in two versions - Magento 1 and Magento 2, as well as two editions called Magento Premium and the open-source version for anyone to use.

Features

This platform offers everything a dropshipping business requires and much more. The quick page loading speed, along with the easy checkout process and catalog page, marketing tools, comprehensive site management, good security, and SEO features, are amongst its noteworthy features.

Time and cost

If you're just starting a dropshipping business, then opt for the free, open-source version. The caveat to this is you need some technical knowledge to develop a dropshipping website. Or, you can hire developers provided by the platform. It can take anywhere between 1 to 3 months and cost you $3000 to $5000.

Ease-of-use

This platform is incredibly user-friendly on the front end, but the backend might be a little complicated for anyone without technical knowledge. However, after spending a little time on this website and going through the user guides provided by Magento, you will get the hang of it.

Scalability and support

It's perhaps the most scalable e-commerce platform available these days. It not only supports small dropshippers who have a fixed number of products, but it also gives your business the support you require to grow. You're free to add unlimited products and catalogs and handle several orders at once. As with WooCommerce, you must install thirdparty plugins to integrate dropshipping functionalities into this platform, and it can cost up to $950.

OpenCart

This is a free e-commerce platform that must be considered by all the new dropshippers. It shares several similarities with Magento, it's available free of cost, it's quite powerful, open-source, and is suitable for beginners, as well as those who are more technically knowledgeable.

Features

It offers a variety of e-commerce functionalities, including support for multiple currencies, the ability to add unlimited products under several category choices, different shipping methods, backup and restore tools, comprehensive sales reports, integrated payment gateways, and more.

Time and cost

You don't have to spend anything to use this platform because it's open-source. You get free support, along with software updates, whenever you use it to create a dropshipping store. So, a significant portion of the costs involved to set up the store will be for hiring designers and developers for setting up the website. It can take anywhere between 2 to 5 months to build a website on this platform.

Ease-of-use

If you have any experience developing websites, this is a great platform. However, it doesn't mean that beginners won't understand the way this platform functions. If you want to set up a dropshipping website, you will need some additional professional help, unless you know how to build the website yourself. As long as you have a good team of developers in place, it's one of the best platforms you can use. Also, the easy and clean user interface is an added advantage.

Scalability and support

Scalability is not one of the benefits of this platform. It's best suited for small- and medium-sized dropshipping businesses. You can contact the support team on this platform, either by creating a ticket or sending an email. Also, you can join its user forum to seek assistance from others. There are different dropshipping extensions. like various plugins, that can be easily integrated with this platform, starting from $99.

Shopify

Shopify has become a popular option for dropshippers. It supports thousands of e-commerce stores. The dropshipping plugin, Oberlo, is an exclusive feature on Shopify. You can use it to find products for your dropshipping business and look at a list of verified suppliers.

Features

There are plenty of useful features provided by this e-commerce platform ranging from various theme settings to management of products, orders, and customers, along with payment options via credit card, unlimited hosting, multiple taxes, optimization for different languages and currencies, SEO and much more.

Time and cost

Unlike the other platforms mentioned so far, there's a fee to use this platform, ranging from \$29 to \$299 per month. If you choose a specific theme, you must pay to use it. There are more than 100 themes available, but only about 10 of them are free to use. Also, Shopify charges a specific amount per sale whenever you integrate other external payment gateways instead of the ones bundled with the platform. One of the advantages of using this e-commerce platform for your dropshipping store is the minimal amount of set-up time required. You can have a store up and running within a couple of hours or days.

Ease-of-use

If you have no technical knowledge or background, this platform is a good option. To create your dropshipping website, start by signing up, select a package, and a theme. After this, it's all about customization.

Scalability and support

This e-commerce platform is easily scalable and can be used to either scale your business up or down by selecting the right package. So, anyone from beginners to larger dropshipping businesses can use this platform. There are various support channels offered by this platform ranging from live chat, email, phone calls, and even forum support.

BigCommerce

There are more than 50,000 e-commerce websites actively working on this platform across the globe. As with Shopify, there are monthly packages available on BigCommerce ranging from $29.95 to $249.95, including transactional fees.

Features

All the essential e-commerce features needed to set up a dropshipping store, like catalog creation, product management, inventory management, marketing features, and payment gateways, are offered by this platform. For shipping, it's integrated with ShipStation and ShipperHQ, and Avalra for tax automation.

Time and cost

There are three packages offered by this e-commerce platform: standard, plus, and pro. It's quite easy to set up a website on this platform. Simply register your account, choose a template, and then start customizing your dropshipping store. Before you decide to buy a specific package, use the 15-day trial period to understand which model is best suited for your business.

Ease-of-use

The best feature of this platform is its ease of use. Even newbies can start using this platform. It's considered to be among the best ecommerce solutions available today. Once you select a proper theme for your website, it's all about customization, which you can do without any prior technical knowledge.

Scalability and support

Since there are various monthly plans, scaling your business isn't difficult while using this e-commerce platform. Choose a package based on the number of products you wish to sell, along with the features you require. You can reach the BigCommerce support team via live chat, email, phone, or even their customer forum.

Chapter 7: Sales Funnels

Stages of a Sales Funnel

As an entrepreneur, your goal is to increase your sales. Ideally, you'd want every visitor to your website to make at least one purchase. In reality, however, this doesn't always happen. We all lead rather hectic lives these days. We're all bombarded with lots of information on a daily basis. Not to mention, there's plenty of competition and choices out there. While you may not always get a sale from a customer's first visit, you can certainly try by introducing them to your sales funnel.

What is a sales funnel?

A sales funnel the path a customer takes from the moment they're aware of your brand/product to the when they make a purchase. Every business has a different type of sales funnel, but they are all based on a similar concept, which can be divided into four stages. They are:

Stage 1: awareness

The customer becomes aware of your brand for the first time. They recognize they have a need to be fulfilled, or a problem to be solved. During this stage, they might find your business. When they see what you're selling, they become interested, but not enough to immediately make a purchase.

Stage 2: interest

After awareness, it's time to get potential buyers hooked onto your business and products. Provide them with engaging, interesting, and valuable content.

The more interest you build for your products, the more likely they are to progress to the next stage of the sales funnel.

Stage 3: desire

In this stage, you already know that your customers are interested in what you have to offer. You need to work on triggering their desire to make a purchase. Your content must provide valuable information about your products, such as the benefits they offer. For example, if you're selling backpacks, instead of listing just the specifications, try putting yourself in the shoes of your audience and describe the backpack's benefits. If readers can visualize using your product, they'll be more inclined to move on to the next and final stage of your sales funnel.

Stage 4: action

It's time to close the sale. At this stage, your only motivation is to get your prospective customers to purchase your product from your website. To do this, your website must be well optimized. For instance, a customer will not purchase if he runs into trouble at the payment stage. Offer various methods of payment and make sure the checkout process is convenient and simple. Navigation and the user interface of your website must also be user-friendly.

The Dropshipping Sales Funnel

Congratulations on getting a step closer to establishing a successful dropshipping business. Now that you're aware of the products you want to sell, the suppliers you want to work with, and the sales platform you're using, you need to make it easy for potential customers to find your store, and you need to get them to buy from you. Every day without traffic to your website is a day of lost revenue. This is why your dropshipping business needs to have an effective sales funnel.

Let's look at the steps you can follow to create a sales funnel for your dropshipping business.

Step #1: Leverage Facebook ads

The brilliance of Facebook ads lies in the feature that allows precise targeting. There are a variety of options you can use to target and attract specific traffic to your website or landing pages.

For now, concentrate on targeting using individual products instead of product categories for driving traffic to your dropshipping store. This is done because you're trying to get traffic to sell products easily and quickly. It's easier to target all those who click on a specific product ad, especially those who click on product-specific ads and are believed to be interested in making a purchase.

Paid traffic plays an important role in the last couple of minutes before a purchase decision is made. It's primarily why you must concentrate on starting a sales funnel and by using Facebook ads.

Open the Facebook ads manager and go to the *Campaigns* tab and click *Create*. If a window pops up prompting you to choose how you wish to create the ad campaign, select guided creation. The next step is to select the campaign goals. Since the idea is to increase sales, choose convergence as your goal. Now it's time to name the campaign. When you've completed these steps, click on *Continue*.

There are five stages in the ad set section: conversion, audience, offer, budget & schedule, and placement. In this section, let's look at conversion and audience. Begin by naming the ad set. Right below this, you will find the conversion option. If you want Facebook to understand what you mean by conversion and effectively track it, you must select a specific conversion, and then set up your pixel to enable Facebook to track the data.

Select the create pixel option and name it. Next, you will notice an option to either install the pixel code yourself or to use one of the assisted methods. If you're using an e-commerce platform, such as WooCommerce or Shopify, be sure to follow that platform's guidelines for installing the pixel code. When you've completed this since you're trying to increase your sales at this stage, select the purchase option.

You can now begin selecting your targeted audience. The first stage is about defining the audience based on their location, gender, age, and language. For instance, if you're selling stylish and affordable watches for women, your target audience might be women who are 18-30 years old, who speak English and are located across the globe.

The next step is to select your target audience's interests, demographics, and behaviors according to the product you're advertising. Sticking with the previous example, there are various factors you can include in women's clothing and fashion accessories while excluding factors like luxury goods (since you're selling affordable watches).

Depending on the figures you've entered, the numbers displayed on the right-hand side of the window will change. You can see the estimated daily reach along with the conversions. Try a couple of options and targeting inputs to see the changes.

The final step is to select your ad budget and its schedule. This decision is entirely up to you and is another factor that influences your overall reach and conversions. Once again, play with some of the inputs until you find a suitable estimate. You can start with a couple of dollars and slowly increase the value.

Select *Continue* and you'll be directed to the final stage in setting up a Facebook ad. Start by selecting the identity that will show in your ads; it can either be an Instagram account or a Facebook page. If your business doesn't have a Facebook page, create one immediately. Select how you want the ad to look; namely, the format of the ad. The simplest ones to start with are the carousel ad or single-image formats.

The final step is to select the images and all the links to be used in the ad. If this is your first ad, then click to enable manually choosing images, links, and videos option to get a feel for how the ad will look after all the specific information is added. (If you don't want to do this, then you can start using the filled template, which uses your Facebook page catalog to create a carousel ad.) If you choose the carousel format, be sure you have at least three sets of links and visuals to go with the ad.

When you've filled in all this information, on the right side you'll see a preview of your ad. You can look at the desktop and mobile versions, as well as the Instagram ad format you want to run. If you're happy with all this, click on confirm. Now your Facebook ads are up and running.

Facebook is quite intuitive and helpful with its step-by-step guidance through the process. It also recommends specifications for images, headlines, and even prompts you to enter the links or URLs when required. All these links will direct your leads to your landing pages.

Step #2: Landing pages

Your ad won't be of much use if you don't have good landing pages. Since the first stage of the sales funnel was to attract the attention of your target audience, the next step is to direct them to the desired location: the product page. This is the bricks-and-mortar equivalent of a store's window display in a mall.

The ads you place online are similar to a store's display window. They offer potential customers a quick peek into the store's product selection it sells. When a potential buyer clicks on a website's ad, it must take them directly to a specific landing page that reflects why they clicked on the ad in the first place.

Visitors to your online store don't want to be misled by advertising. Before you start selling a specific product, make sure you've obtained samples from the supplier. Use photos of these samples and place them on the website. Use at least three high-quality, zoomable images of the products. If there are any variants available for the same product, don't forget to include those images as well. If possible, use photos of the product from multiple angles.

The product description is also one aspect you cannot overlook because it bridges the gap between the product and the potential customer. Since the customers cannot physically test a product before purchasing it online, the description should detail its features, its uses and the materials it's made of. You can always repurpose information provided by the manufacturer or the supplier, but it creates more impact when you add your personal touch, particularly when it appeals to your target audience. Take the time to see the product from your customer's perspective; answer at least a couple of questions a potential buyer might have.

Start the product description with a short and simple paragraph, followed by a bullet list of features and benefits.

Remember to include details about shipping and pricing on the product page. While it may be self-explanatory, don't overlook the fact that no one would be interested in hunting for the exact price of the product on your dropshipping store. Many buyers tend to back out of a purchase due to shipping costs. Be as transparent as you possibly can about this. Decision-making certainly becomes easier when all the information is easy to understand and readily available.

Include some real reviews. You obviously won't have any reviews at the start. However, once you start selling, it becomes easier to display social proof of the products you sell by showing ratings and reviews given by other customers.

Try to anticipate the different types of questions you might receive about the product and create a list of frequently asked questions (FAQs). To increase your sales, you must have a strong product page, or you risk customers getting turned off and leaving without having made a purchase.

Step #3: Concentrate on abandoned carts

There are times when a potential customer wants to buy your product, but for whatever reason, backs out of the process, abandoning the item in their shopping cart. It's not the end of the road for that customer. You still have an opportunity to gently nudge them into becoming a paying customer.

The simplest and most effective time to do this is when their purchase intent is at its highest--when they've added products to their shopping cart.

After capturing their information, the best strategy is to add it to your email list and engage with them directly. Since the customer has already added products to the cart, the purchase intention is quite high. A simple message or an email reminder might be all the nudge required to complete the sale.

If you want to do this, you must start by setting up a system for collecting their information. *Recart* is one such integration you can use to collect email addresses while reminding potential customers to complete the sale they left in their cart.

The next step is to create and customize certain messages or emails depending on various channels. You can send cart reminders via email, messenger reminders, or even a simple push notification. However, in crafting your message, keep in mind the environment the customer views the message. For example, a mobile push notification requires a much shorter note than an email viewed on a computer.

Subtly remind the potential customers of the products left in their cart and how quickly they can complete their purchase. The final step is to send the message within one to four hours from the moment the customer abandoned the cart.

Once you've established your dropshipping sales funnel, the next thing to focus on is increasing the average order value. This refers to increasing the amount of money a potential customer will spend on your dropshipping store. You can do this by making complementary product recommendations based on their cart contents. If you've ever shopped on Amazon, you'll see several of these recommendations before making your purchase. It's an effective way to introduce new products to customers while gently nudging them to increase their cart value.

Consider all the products that go well together. For example, if you're selling bedside lamps, you can provide lightbulb recommendations; or if you're selling clothing, you can include accessories. Once you start selling, you may notice some of your products selling better than others. Always recommend popular products whenever they are related to the ones already in your customer's cart.

Be mindful of the number of options you provide. If you overwhelm the customer with too many choices, it won't be as effective. For instance, if a customer adds a dress to the shopping cart, offering recommendations for dozens of other blouses, shoes, and accessories won't make any sense. It might actually discourage the customer from going through the recommendations. Instead, offer from three to four recommendations for a quicker purchase decision.

Now that you're aware of what a dropshipping sales funnel means and the three steps to follow, it's time to set up a sales funnel! Whatever amount you incur on advertising and marketing is merely an investment made to earn higher revenues. The great thing about Facebook ads is that you can decide how much you wish to spend and customize the duration of the ad you run. So, start creating your sales funnel immediately to increase your sales.

Chapter 8: Customer Service

Customer satisfaction must be a priority if you want to become a successful dropshipper. If the customer is happy after a sale, the chances of repeat purchases will increase. A little extra time, money, and effort are required to offer excellent customer service. Don't compromise on these things, because in the long run, they help establish a loyal customer base for your business.

Good customer service is also a way to increase positive word-ofmouth publicity. Regardless of all the fancy marketing techniques you use, never underestimate the power of good old-fashioned word-ofmouth. When a customer is happy with the service you provide, the chances of them recommending your business to others will increase.

Respect

A cardinal rule of customer service is to treat your customers with respect. Even if the customer is not reciprocating, be respectful. Learning to deal with even the most troublesome of customers is a useful skill. Be patient and calm while addressing any of their issues. A little respect goes a long way. In fact, it might also turn an angry customer into a loyal one.

Get Feedback

Obtaining feedback is important, regardless of whether it's positive or negative. Feedback helps you gauge the level of customer satisfaction and it's an opportunity to show good customer service. It gives you an idea about the areas of your business you need to improve upon and the ones at which you're excelling.

Obtain feedback after you've completed the sale. If you receive positive feedback, quickly respond to it and thank the customer. If it's negative feedback, follow up with them immediately to understand what you can do to improve.

After-Sales Service

Some businesses tend to forget a customer right after the sale. This might be true if all you're focusing on is a one-time purchase. However, if you're in it for the long haul, then consider the after-sales service you provide as well. Inform your customers that their continued support is invaluable and that you appreciate their business. Any after-sales service gives you the chance to introduce more products. You can convert your current customers into repeat customers by providing good after-sales service. Stay in touch by sending regular and consistent emails to them about all the products your business has to offer.

Complaints

Dealing with customer complaints is an integral part of running a business. You must deal with any complaint as positively as possible. Listen carefully to your customer's grievance and address them appropriately and immediately. Don't think of customer complaints as a setback, but an opportunity to learn and improve your business.

Returns

There will be times when a customer returns their purchase. Whatever the reason, you must have a procedure in place to deal with returns. If the product the customer received is defective, replace it immediately. Always provide your return policies and guidelines on your website. You and your supplier must decide on the return policy together.

Empathy and Listening Skills

While dealing with customers, always be empathetic. Learning to be (or appearing to be) empathetic is a useful skill in all aspects of your business. By showing empathy, you can create a positive bond between the business and the customer. It can also make the customer feel welcome.

When dealing with a customer, be a good listener. If you don't listen to the issue, you can't possibly address it adequately. Regardless of what your customer has to say, listen patiently and carefully. This means you have to understand what they're trying to convey.

Good Rapport

Establishing a good rapport with your customers helps ensure that your customers stick around and remember your business for future purchases. It also allows you to highlight any shared interests and passions to make the business seem more personable. Keep in mind that a happy customer is an invaluable asset to your business. If they're satisfied with the service you provide, they'll become loyal to the business. A loyal customer base will always help you stand out from your competitors.

Set Standards

Establish customer service standards for everyone to follow. It's not just about drafting rules and forgetting about them. Following them is just as important. Failure to do so can create significant setbacks. Draft a document detailing how to handle customers. These standards will ensure you and your employees are dealing with customers appropriately.

Learn to manage customers' expectations by communicating to them what you can or cannot do for them. If you make promises, always follow through. Avoid committing to anything you have no intention of keeping. Ensure all your business standards, along with policies, are clearly stated in the description of the items or products you sell on the website.

Include FAQs

Another critical aspect of customer service is including easily-found FAQs on your website. Customers will have questions about your business, and by creating these pages, those questions can be answered immediately. There will be times when customers are confused about common information such as billing, delivery, or even shipping. Address all these issues in your FAQs. Remember to include contact information if a customer has a question not addressed in your FAQs page.

Your Team

If you have team members working with you or if you have employees on the payroll, you must learn to value them. Your employees are your first customers. If you don't maintain good relations with your employees, they won't want to work for you. If your employees are happy, they'll provide better service to your customers. Every aspect of customer service is interconnected, and ignoring even one of these aspects can harm your business.

By following the different tips and strategies given in this section, you can develop a good relationship with your existing and potential customers.

Chapter 9: Email Lists

Remember to consider local privacy laws with regard to electronic communication. They may differ from country to country.

An email list includes the names and email addresses of all those who have provided explicit permission for you to send contact them with updates and promotional offers related to your business.

Many people underestimate the power of creating an email list, especially at the beginning stages. If you're interested in successfully marketing your business, you must leave no stone unturned. In this section, you will learn about the various advantages of building an email list and the different steps to follow to create one.

Email is quite personal. Even if you send them to hundreds of users, each email is personal. It gives you direct access to the inbox of your target audience. Unlike other social media platforms, you don't have to worry about any ranking system related to the way the emails are displayed. Since the user has already shown interest in your business, it becomes easier to market your products to them.

It's safe to say that email is one of the best methods of targeted marketing. Since you're already aware of customer preferences, it's easier to cater to their needs and create content specifically targeted to them.

With email, if your targeted customer has any questions about your products or services, they can immediately email you about it. This, in turn, creates a bond between your business and your customers.

A study conducted by the Radicati Group estimated there to be more than 3.8 billion active email accounts across the globe. This number is far higher than the number of active accounts on Instagram and Facebook combined.

So, it would be foolish to ignore a brilliant opportunity as targeted and as large as email.

When you send a business-related email to your customers, such as a newsletter or a product update, include a signup button. Alternatively, you can also add a link directing users to sign up for your email list. Whenever someone on your recipient list forwards the email to someone else, they can easily sign up using the link or the button. To increase this sharing, offer valuable content in your emails.

The first point of contact for a lot of people who are interested in purchasing products from your business is the official website. Always include a signup form on your website.

Another great way to increase the number of subscribers on your email list is to attend industry trade shows, conferences, workshops, or other business-related events. It gives you a chance to interact with other professionals and potential customers.

Don't forget about your existing list of contacts like current/former colleagues, family members, friends, acquaintances, or anyone else you know. Even if, during the initial phases, your email list includes only personal contacts, it's okay. It's a way to get started. You can obtain feedback from all these people and make the necessary changes before you proceed. You can also use your personal contacts to promote your business and spread the word about your products.

Provide valuable content on your websites, such as articles or blog posts related to content you think your targeted audience would enjoy. This not only keeps your audience engaged, but it's also a great way to grow your email list. If you're providing an interesting article, then you can include an additional request for contact information if readers/customers want to be kept informed of future content.

You can start using lead magnets for growing your customer relationships. Lead magnets include free downloadable white papers or other educational resources in exchange for email addresses. When doing this, offer unique and engaging content. It must be resourceful as well as entertaining to your audience. You can offer them a sample of the white paper and then prompt them to sign up to your email list for full access.

Your business website must be optimized not just for computers, but also for smartphones. Because of how popular smartphones have become, it's time to leverage them to grow your email list. You can encourage your existing and potential customers to join your email list by making your website mobile optimized. You can also use a service like Constant Contact or other text-to-join tools to add more names to your email list. By sending a text message with a code unique to your business, you're making it easier for your audience to get onto your email list.

With the popularity of social media around the world, start making the most of your accounts to further your business goals. Regardless of whether it's Facebook, Instagram, or even Twitter, always include a link to your signup page or your homepage. This technique works best when your content is unique, informative and entertaining. If you have an impressive profile on social media, the likelihood of your audience actively joining your email list will also increase.

The concept of exclusivity is always appealing. The more exclusive something is or seems, the more it becomes desired. If you're offering something interesting to your audience, and they can't find elsewhere, it will act as a trigger to compel them to subscribe to your email list. For example, if you're running a discount or sale on your website, you can create a condition that these offers will only be available to those who join your email list.

All the steps discussed in this section are quite simple and practical. So, what are you waiting for? Start implementing these strategies right away and increase your email list of subscribers!

Chapter 10: Increase Leads to Your Dropshipping Store

A lead is someone who expresses interest in the products or services a business offers but is not yet a buyer. Using a marketing strategy to trigger customer interest with the goal of converting them into paying customers is known as lead generation. A potential buyer becomes a lead the moment you start communicating with them. All leads are unique, but there are certain similarities they all share.

For example, if you sell home décor and you get 10 signups to receive your monthly newsletter, if seven of those 10 are renovating their homes and the rest are just doing research, the first set of seven signups are your leads.

As a dropshipper, establishing a store is the first step in getting started in the right direction. Once the store is up and running, you need plenty of traffic to increase your sales. This section will look at some practical and effective ways to increase your leads.

Search Engine Optimization (SEO)

SEO primarily deals with tools and techniques to increase your website's online visibility. It helps to boost the quality and quantity of traffic to your dropshipping store through organic search engine results.

Whenever you search for something on Yahoo, Google, Bing, or other search engines, you get hundreds of hits. How do these platforms display the results? Search engines have crawlers that gather all information about specific online content. Results are fed into the search engine to build an index by the crawlers.

These indexes run through an algorithm (a fancy mathematical equation) that matches all available data with the quality results you're looking to find. From keywords used to product features, regular traffic, link features, these are just some of the factors the algorithm uses to match the ranking of the search results.

It's a complicated process behind the scenes, but SEO can be rather simple. From including title tags to meta descriptions and promoting the right links, you can optimize the dropshipping store for better SEO your results.

One way to improve the visibility of your dropshipping store is by creating a blog. If not, you can start a blog on WordPress, or even use WooCommerce or BigCommerce. In your blog, post valuable information your audience might enjoy. It's a subtle way to market your dropshipping store without hard selling.

Adding a blog isn't the only way to optimize search results. You can also optimize individual pages of your dropshipping store for better online visibility. The one page you must always optimize is the product page. By doing this, your products show up easily on the search engines whenever a user types the name of a specific product.

The content of the website must be thoroughly engaging and entertaining. It must not be a reproduction of information that is already available. If that's the case, then the ranking of your site will never increase. This strategy is known as content marketing. All the titles and tags you use for the dropshipping business must be attractive. A search engine tends to use these titles as the title of a book. It means the stacks essentially describe the content available, so ensure that you make it count. All the h1 tags must include a short description between four to six words.

Use quality meta descriptions to improve search results. It means those who view the metadata are deciding whether to click on the result or not. So, if the meta tag is attractive, the user might consider it. It needs to be between 130 to 150 characters and not more than that. You can look at the meta tags used by your competitors and come up with a similar one for your dropshipping store.

Another way to improve the search engine ranking is by finding backlinks. The more content you create, the easier it is for others to recommend your articles on other websites. When this happens, it creates a backlink. So, work on creating good content for your social media profiles, as well as any blogs you maintain.

The Google algorithm can index a website efficiently when you have a sitemap for your dropshipping store. A site map essentially shows all the different pages or the list of pages your website offers at a glance.

Pay-Per-Click Advertising (PPC)

Pay-per-click is a form of online advertising that charges the advertiser only when the ad is clicked and they're directed to the advertiser's website. The advertising on Google are examples of pay-per-click. SEO, when combined with PPC, makes for a great marketing strategy. The biggest PPC ad platform is Google (Google ads and Google shopping).

The daily budget for a PPC strategy can range anywhere from $5 to $5,000 depending on your marketing capacity. While using Google AdWords, you must select keywords you wish to target. By targeting these keywords, whenever a user searches for it, your Google ads will show up. For example, if you sell baby clothing, your target keywords can be "baby clothing", "baby gifts", "baby shoes", or even long-tailed keywords like "organic" and "soft baby clothing".

Consider using Google shopping, which is often referred to as product listing ads. These ads are usually shown at the top. When someone searches for a specific product on Google, it can also be found through the shopping tab on Google.

Try using other search engines as well. Any Google ad you plan to run can be imported into Bing ads. If a majority of your target audience uses Bing, diversify your marketing strategy.

Build Trust

Shoppers can be skeptical about the quality of dropshipping products. To increase customer trust, add ratings, customer reviews, and testimonials. Product reviews give new visitors an idea of the experience previous buyers have had with your business. It might be a motivating factor nudging a potential buyer to a paid customer. For example, different dropshipping owners on AliExpress take snapshots of customer feedback and post it to their websites.

Social Videos

A significant portion of consumer web traffic comes from social videos. You can drive traffic to your dropshipping store by sharing social videos that promote your products or simply to expand awareness of your brand. For example, posting previews and how-to videos, or tutorials on your social media accounts is a great way to direct your target audience to your dropshipping website. For a smallscale dropshipping business, creating engaging social videos might be more of a challenge, so if you're skeptical about creating engaging content on your own, you can always look for existing viral videos on popular sites and share them on your media profiles. While doing this, don't forget to share the post with an effective call-to-action that quickly drives traffic to your dropshipping website.

Remember the Niche

Spend some time identifying the different online platforms and communities on which your niche might spend their time, and then join them so you can engage with your targeted customers. You can also see the topics your usual audience discusses and you can act as a brand ambassador to subtly promote your dropshipping business or introduce new products to members in this niche. You can even behave like a user and make yourself an expert in the given niche. The groups and social media pages can also be targeted for featuring your dropshipping business. For instance, if your dropshipping business is about shoes, you can send fashion looks, and ask the group members to post them on the group page by tagging your dropshipping store.

Blog Marketing

Blog marketing is a low-cost and effective strategy to reach your customers. The primary benefit of blog marketing is that it allows you to build your target audience and create more traffic and leads to your dropshipping business and it also improves your SEO results. The more streamlined your blog posts are with your website content and SEO, the higher your website's ranking in the search engine's results. The better your website's ranking, the easier it will be for shoppers to find your dropshipping business. However, to do this, ensure that you're creating and curating worthy content that your target audience will enjoy. If the content created is not in sync or related to the website or the dropshipping business, the audience will quickly lose interest.

Email Pop-Ups

A majority of visitors tend to leave a website within 15 seconds of opening a website. It's important to use that short timespan to capture a visitor's email address, ideally to improve your lead conversion. One way to do this is by using an email pop-up to ask them to join your email list. Once you've captured their information, if you have an outreach system in place, you can nurture relationships with visitors to your site with the goal of turning them into paid customers. There are different third-party services you can use, like Better Coupon Box, to customize email pop-ups that help grow your email subscriber list. At times, customers might get annoyed with all these pop-ups. Therefore, it's quintessential that the email pop-ups you set don't disrupt the visitor's shopping flow.

Customer Retargeting

Customer retargeting is an effective strategy for people who have visited your site previously but didn't take any action. You can display relevant ads to all such visitors by using retargeting. These ads help reinforce the previous motivations a prospective buyer had and help nudge them in the right direction.

Cluster your visitors into different segments, such as product page visitors, recent buyers, visitors who have abandoned carts, and homepage visitors. Classify them based on the time of the visit. The intent of a visitor who browses your website last week will be different than someone who did so yesterday. Order them according to the recency of their visits. Then consider the different online platforms you can use to retarget them. You can use Facebook ads, Google AdWords, or even a combination of these two things to make your retargeting strategy more effective.

Upselling

Upselling is a technique used to recommend relevant or better or alternative products. When a customer adds an item to their cart, a pop-up appears showing a list of other complementary products available for purchase.

Who doesn't like attractive offers or discounts? One of the most obvious and efficient ways to attract your target audience is by offering free trials, discounts, and other attractive offers. The likelihood of customers making instant and repeat purchases increases whenever there are good promotions available. You can use a WooCommerce plugin like Boost Sales to make upselling easier.

Chapter 11: Tips for Beginners

Web Pages

Positive customer experience must be your priority if you want to be a successful dropshipping e-commerce store owner. There are a couple of important pages every dropshipping website must include. They are: about us, contact, return and exchange policies, featured products, shipping details, FAQs, privacy policies, terms and conditions for warranty, size guide (where applicable), and customer support.

Homepage

Your website essentially acts as the storefront for your dropshipping business. So, the web pages you include must provide all the information a potential buyer might need.

On the homepage, you must include your brand's story and information about what your business does. This page must be captivating and engaging. You cannot include generic information -- make it specific to your business. That said, all the information must be presented in a crisp and easy to read format. The page must include a clear value proposition, offers simple navigation, high-quality images, a call to action, and contact information.

Since your primary idea is to increase your sales, the first thing the user sees on the homepage should ideally be the required action you want them to take. By giving them an eye-popping call to action and then guiding them to take the desired action, you can increase your sales.

For instance, you can feature one of your best-selling products on the homepage with a simple call to action like, "Grab them before they're gone," or something similar. Don't forget to include a button to direct the user to the relevant product page. Avoid overcrowding this page with unnecessary information.

Product page

When it comes to an online storefront, a product page is very important. On the product page, include all the details about the products your dropshipping store offers. Regardless of how brilliant your products are, you cannot increase your sales if your product pages are poorly crafted.

Some of the important elements of a product page are product titles, high-quality images, product videos, call-to-action buttons, product reviews, and product descriptions.

You cannot have a product page without effective product titles. Ensure the titles are easy to read and don't exceed 7-10 words. Keep in mind that you can describe the product in the product descriptions.

Ensure that the product descriptions list out all the necessary information and details like product specifications, ideal use, features, and product highlights. Once you've been in the business for a while, you can start adding product reviews as well.

If you just have one category of products, then you don't need product categories. However, if there are multiple categories, then you must think about creating product category pages. It ensures that users don't have to go through a ton of information before finding what they are looking for. For instance, if you're dropshipping apparel for men, women, and children, then you should create at least three category pages to cater to each of these product categories.

Privacy policy

Your website's privacy policy informs all the users about the data your website collects, and how this data is used by your business. It provides different information about how data is collected, whether it's by a form or even cookies on the website. You cannot start collecting user data without giving them prior notice. It could be something as simple as a popup that says, "This website uses cookies to gather user data."

There are various regulations about data privacy popping up these days and unnecessary lawsuits. If you want to avoid any legal hassles, then you must include this page. Don't get discouraged thinking about all the laws you have to review. There are plenty of free and paid online tools you can use for creating your site's privacy policy. For instance, a website like freeprivacypolicy.com does all this for you. You can always hire a legal professional for help in creating a privacy policy and terms of use.

FAQ page

The FAQ page, as the name suggests, must answer some of the common questions a potential user might have before making a purchase. Include details about shipping, returns, refunds, payment methods, and any other information about the products you can think of. You can look at your competitor's websites to get a better idea of all the information that must be included on your business website.

Contact us

This is one page you cannot overlook while creating your dropshipping business. The contact us page provides all the contact information about your business.

Since it's an online store, there will be no face-to-face interaction. So, if the user needs to get in touch with your business, he will need some information about this. Include a phone number, email address, P.O.

Box address, and the physical location of the store or office (if there is one).

Also, include the operation hours of the business. Remember to reply to all emails and phone calls you receive. The contact us page not only allows the potential users to contact your business, but it also enables Google to find your business information in the local metadata you include.

Terms of use

For any online storefront, you need to have a well-drafted agreement stating all the terms and conditions. Have this page clearly linked on your website, and easily accessible.

The terms and conditions agreement essentially protects your business from unnecessary legal issues. It also details the different sets of rules that apply to you and the customers who make a purchase, and it helps limit your liability in case of a conflict. If you don't have any legal background, it's ideal that you hire a professional to help you draft the terms and conditions agreement.

Note: These are just some of the pages you can include. It is not an exhaustive list.

Online and Offline

Social media is certainly quite important for any e-commerce store, and especially dropshipping business owners. However, it's not the only channel your brand must use actively. Spend a little time and research about video marketing and try to take an active part in all those events wherein you know your target audience will be in attendance. Go through different social media profiles and find influencers in your niche.

If the products you offer can be of some advantage to the influencer, then you might be able to partner with them. Learn to be innovative and never stop learning when it comes to dropshipping. Your business must be seen not just online, but also offline if you want to be an effective and successful dropshipper.

Offline or guerilla marketing is another great way to increase your business visibility. The offline marketing strategies you use will depend on your target market and the products you offer.

Regardless of what you do, all your marketing efforts must communicate your business' unique value proposition. The power of human interaction can never be underestimated. Even if you're an online business, by delivering a brilliant offline experience, you can set yourself apart from the rest of the competitors in the market.

If possible, and if you have the resources, different types of offline marketing you can opt for include trunk shows, pop-up shops, flyers, postcards, and most importantly, word of mouth publicity.

Flyers might sound a little old-fashioned, but they certainly help draw attention to your business. You can post flyers in public places such as supermarkets, restaurants, cafes, or any other locations you can think of. However, before you do this, check to ensure you're not breaking any rules or regulations. Seek permission before you do this.

You might have experienced a pop-up shop as a customer. It's time to recreate the same experience for your potential customers. As the name suggests, it's a temporary stall or shop. It usually lasts for a day or two and is quite similar to setting up a stall at a trade show. To do this, you must have some inventory available. It's a great way to personally market products and your business to potential customers. You can easily set up a pop-up shop in a restaurant, street corner, cafe, office, or even inside another store. Before you do this, you must always get permission.

A trunk show is quite similar to a trade show. Unlike a trade show, which is essentially B2B, a trunk show allows you to interact with your potential customers or other interested parties.

Trustworthy Brand

When it comes to dropshipping, the responsibility to present your business depends on you. If you strengthen your brand's positioning in the market, it helps improve your reputation as a brand leader.

Take some time and think about all the aspects or features that make your business unique, and concentrate on the ones that help strengthen your brand image. Customers love to purchase products from brands they trust. So, by building brand awareness and improving your brand's image, you can gain your customer's trust. Your brand image is your business' personality that is visible to your target audience.

To create a trustworthy brand, you must be transparent. This ensures that your customers know you're operating an honest business. So, be transparent about your business policies and mention all the essential details in the different web pages on your website.

Ensure that all the information is unambiguous and easy to understand. There are various ways in which potential and existing customers might try to contact your business. Regardless of whether they reach you via social media, your customer service portal, or even the phone, answer all their questions. This helps build trust since your customers cannot physically visit your storefront to clarify their doubts.

Another simple way to do this is by not just understanding your customers, but also demonstrating that you have understood their needs. Start by examining all the customer data you collect. Practice social listening by monitoring all the online conversations your audience might have about your business or the concerned industry. This enables you to assess how others perceive your business.

Don't forget to ask for feedback. Even if you think you've done a marvelous job, others might have different opinions. Getting all these opinions allows you to improve your existing business practices.

Try to get more personalized with your customers. Using a one size fits all email marketing campaign is certainly easier, but it's quite impersonal. To do this, you must ask them for feedback after a sale is complete, answer their questions on social media, and respond to any of their requests.

Another effective tactic for establishing trust is the way you respond to criticism. Regardless of whether a customer has a question, a random doubt, or any negative feedback, they always expect prompt responses from businesses. By offering a prompt response, it shows the customer your willingness to help them. Don't worry about criticism, and try to address customer concerns.

High-Quality Content

Potential consumers tend to go through hundreds of websites not just to obtain the information, but also to understand all their options. If they're searching for a specific product to purchase, and if you keep running into the same information over and over again, it can be a little frustrating. So, be sure you have the necessary information and content about every product your business sells. You must also mention it on your e-commerce website. When you update your product listing, don't forget to update the listing on your dropshipping store as well. Always use high-quality images and content for this purpose. The content you offer must be valuable. If not, it will get lost in all the background noise.

Holidays

Use holidays to offer promotions, discounts and other special offers to customers. For example, Black Friday is considered a huge sales bonanza for most of North America. It's not just for brick and mortar stores; online businesses can also get in on the action! Remember to include notable holidays from other geographies as well.

Returns

A couple of areas you cannot afford to overlook include returns or refunds, claims of lost shipments, and backorders. These issues become a little tricky for dropshippers since they don't have any direct control over product processing, packaging, order processing, and shipment. Since these are potential problems, creating a contingency plan can help you to avoid them.

The simplest way to resolve return claims is to ask customers to send the returned items directly to you. By doing this, it not only gives you greater control over the customer experience, it also enables you to provide customer service. However, the downside is that you require plenty of logistics for reselling, receiving, and storage.

The good news is, most suppliers usually have a return policy in place. If you decide to work with such policies, then the customers' return items are going directly to the supplier. So, you don't have to worry about the previously stated logistics.

However, there are certain problems associated with this idea. The supplier can reject the returned items if they aren't shipped on time or in good condition. You might have to pay certain extra fees to the supplier whenever the items are returned. Apart from that, you also have an obligation as a vendor. Therefore, you must always discuss the return policy with the supplier and make sure you have everything in writing. An agreement can go a long way when it comes to securing and protecting your business interests in e-commerce.

While developing the return policy, first talk to your suppliers about their return policy. Then create a return policy that matches the one your supplier has. For instance, if your supplier has a 15-day return policy, then your return policy must be about 5-10 days and no more.

If it exceeds this time limit, your supplier will not accept the return. Before you start framing the return policy, start thinking about the common reasons (wrong size, wrong product, poor quality, item didn't match the description) why a product might be returned.

Profit Margins

Whenever you select a specific product to list in your store, consider the profit margins. Because profit margins differ from product to product and manufacturer to manufacturer, it can critically affect your bottom line.

Analyze whether the chosen niche will work well for your product's marketing potential, along with the competitiveness involved and the capacity to make profits. Never overprice or underprice products. Since a dropshipper gets all products at wholesale prices, it's important that you consider the profit margin involved.

A simple formula to calculate your profit margin is as follows:

Profit margin = (total sales - total expenses)/total sales

For instance, if your dropshipping businesses manage to sell 20 products for revenue of $500, then your total sales will be $500.

Now, take into consideration all the costs incurred for making the sale. You will include the cost to source the product from the supplier, marketing costs, business costs, or any other fees or charges payable for a hosting service you use. Let's assume that all these costs add up to $350. By using the formula mentioned above, your profit margin will be as follows.

Profit margin = ($500 - $350)/$500

Profit margin = 0.3 x 100

Profit margin = 30%

Once you've calculated your profit margin, look at your overall profitability and decide the markup you wish to include on the product. By increasing the product markup, you can gradually increase your profits.

To estimate the product markup, divide the total cost of acquiring the product by the gross profit you earn on the product. By using the previous example, ($150/$350) x 100, will give you the product markup of 42%.

Note: This is just an example, and it isn't conclusive. Keep in mind that the product offerings cannot be extremely inflated. Product prices must be competitive. So, start crunching some numbers until you find the sweet spot!

Potential Customer Engagement

Understand where your targeted audience spends most of their time and start targeting those platforms. Keep in mind that as a business, you're supposed to reach out to your targeted audience, and it doesn't work the other way around. At least not until you've established yourself as a popular brand. Once you identify the niche, along with the platform, make the most of it. Use it to connect with others who share similar interests as your business.

The idea of customer engagement marketing is relatively new, but it's steadily gaining importance. It's all about delivering calculated, relevant, and personalized messages at the right time to a prospective or an existing customer. For instance, imagine you're checking your inbox and you find a message from a specific online store you recently purchased a product from. The message is sent by the store to inform you about sales, offers, or new products. If you've had any experience with online shopping, then you might have received such messages.

The best way to improve customer engagement is through customer relationship management.

You can also check your existing customer engagement by analyzing the guest checkout rates, average order value, purchase frequency, customer lifetime value, and churn and retention rates. If the guest checkout rate is quite low, it means customers are browsing through the website and creating accounts with your dropshipping website. If the purchase frequency is high, it means your store is able to engage with them and you have returning customers. If the average order value is high, it means customers are developing a sense of loyalty towards your business. If the churn/retention rates are low, it means you have some committed customers.

Simple ways you can concentrate on increasing your customer engagement is by starting a blog and then adding information about this blog to your business website. Start selling the benefits of the product instead of the product itself. You can use the product page and category page for providing relevant information to your audience. If your audience can see the different benefits they stand to gain from the products, their willingness to make a purchase also increases. You must always have a value proposition in mind. The website design must essentially tell all the users about what your business has to offer. So, your website design must stand out while effectively delivering your brand's message to them.

Learn from Mistakes

Success is not possible without some failures. Whenever you make any mistakes or experience failures, don't think of it as the end of the road. It's merely an opportunity for you to learn and improve. The good thing is, you don't necessarily have to learn from your own mistakes or failures; you can learn a lot from the mistakes made by others. You're not the first dropshipper and certainly not the last.

Carefully go through the different mistakes you must avoid that have been mentioned in the previous chapters of this book and try to avoid them. There are some great lessons, provided you're willing to learn.

Here are a couple of mistakes that can damage your dropshipping business. Carefully go through them and see whether you can improve or avoid making any of these mistakes.

The list of common mistakes includes carelessly selecting the niche, a complicated website structure, false discount offers, suspicious reviews, a suspicious number of orders, a lack of social network accounts, unsupervised social media profiles, and incorrect promotion links.

Once your dropshipping businesses are up and running, you must constantly monitor it. Keep a record of all the feedback you receive from customers and suppliers. Carefully analyze different metrics associated with your business website, like the rate of conversion, engagement, customer retention, and so on. There are various online tools you can use to track these metrics. Also, concentrate on the metrics from any of your social media advertising and marketing campaigns.

The different metrics you must track are website traffic, the conversion rate, customer acquisition cost, total sales, shopping cart abandonment rate, average customer order value, and the customer lifetime value. Here are a couple of online tools you can use to track all these metrics.

- KISSmetrics

- Metrilo

- RetentionGrid

- Clicky

- Adobe Marketing Cloud

- Google Analytics

- Crazy Egg

It's not just about tracking these metrics, you must also keep a detailed record of all these metrics. Try to notice any patterns or variations in them. You can use this data to change your marketing strategy or even product offerings. For instance, if you notice that the rate of shopping cart abandonment is quite high, it means you must look at ways in which you can optimize the website to ensure that the user makes the purchase.

Similarly, if you notice that the source of the traffic to your website is high from a social media platform when compared to other sources, then it's time to rethink your marketing strategy. You can redesign the strategy to concentrate more of your efforts on the platform that's providing more traffic. Start making a note of all these insights in a journal or even create an online document for it. If you want, you can also discuss these with your business partners.

Use Social Media to Promote Your Store

It can be easy to get overwhelmed about the various factors you must consider while running a successful social media marketing campaign to promote your dropshipping business. To do this, you must keep up with all the upcoming trends, as well as updates to any algorithms. Apart from that, you must also understand your target audience and social media platforms to use. To make things easier for you, here are some simple tips you can start using to promote your dropshipping store.

Collaboration

Start collaborating with influencers to increase your online presence. Influencers are perhaps your best option for promoting your dropshipping business. Since they operate on several social media channels and have a massive follower base, it makes sense for your brand and your products to collaborate with their profiles. One platform you can use to find influencers according to their specific niche is Influence.co. Alternatively, you can also go through your competitor's social media profiles and see the different influencers (if any) they have collaborated with.

Automation

The world of social media is overcrowded with influencers, users, and plenty of businesses. Because of all this, it's quite easy for your followers to forget about your business unless they are constantly reminded about it.

When constant reminders keep popping up on their social media feeds, the chances of engagement increase. A common problem plenty of ecommerce store owners face is the lack of time and consistency. If you're dealing with the same issue, there's a simple solution -- automation. By using automation tools, the work you might have spent hours on can be completed within minutes.

A popular automation tool for social media management is Buffer. You can create and then pre-set publishing schedules for different social media profiles using this tool. Depending upon your social media schedule, the post can be sent automatically at a specific time and date. By using social automation tools, you can ensure that you don't miss out on new opportunities to post relevant content. It also reduces the chances of over posting while making it easier for you to engage with your target audience.

Engagement

Social media is certainly the perfect channel for engaging with your potential audience while promoting your dropshipping business. However, to do this, create business profiles for your dropshipping business on different social media platforms. For instance, whenever someone tags your business on any of the social media networks, don't forget to reply or comment on such a post. Building a good relationship with your potential customers is a great way to increase your online visibility.

Relatable content

The content you post on social media must not only be of high quality but needs to be relatable too. If the content is irrelevant, you will quickly lose your followers. At times, all that you need is relatable content to spark your potential customer's attention.

The content you create must be suitable for the platforms you use. Not just that, you need to keep in mind the preferences of your audience whenever you're creating content. If the content doesn't appeal to your audience, what's the point of social media marketing?

For instance, the kind of content you would create for YouTube would be quite different from the content you create for Instagram. You can certainly cross-promote your brand on different platforms, but try to use different content as well. Repurposing your content up to a certain extent is permissible, but avoid posting the same content across various channels. It's quite likely that the people who follow you on one platform will be following you on the other platforms as well. If they notice that you keep posting the same content everywhere, you'll quickly lose their interest.

To create relatable content, carefully look through your product offering. Consider your niche and industry. Now, think about the different topics your target audience might be interested in. For instance, if you're dropshipping clothes, you can add articles and blogs about fashion, style, styling tips, and so on. There's plenty of information available online.

You must decide what will appeal to your audience and include it accordingly. You can promote this content on your social media platforms or offer them in your newsletters. However, don't forget to relate all this information to your business website and products. If you curate content about the latest fashion trends, you can include a link to similar products your website offers. It's an effective way to promote your business while providing value to customers.

Product videos

Social media has certainly revolutionized the way businesses operate these days. Social networking sites like Instagram and Facebook allow longer videos that you can use to promote your product, as well as ecommerce stores and interactive and creative ways.

For example, you can publish detailed videos about the product along with tutorials of how the products can be used. By using product videos, you can narrate a short yet valuable story for your target audience that makes them feel like they are interacting with a human and not just a faceless brand. It's also a great way to display your business's personality online.

The simplest product video you can create is a how-to or a tutorial. Go through some tutorials on YouTube to get a better idea of all that you can include. For example, if the product you're dropshipping needs assembly, provide a video guide customers can use to assemble the product. Ensure that it's a high-quality video.

Bonus Gifts

If your dropshipping business sells high-ticket items, you can increase your overall convergence by offering simple bonus gifts with every purchase. Carefully consider your profit margins before you do this.

MAP (minimum advertised price) policies prevent you from offering specific items below this price to beat your competitors. Even if you cannot offer a product at a lower price, you can offer an additional free product with it. By offering more, you can effectively convince your potential audience to buy from your business instead of your competitors.

To offer bonus products, ask yourself what your customers would need or want. Then, take into consideration how expensive it would be for your business. For instance, you might have received a phone case when you purchase a new phone. Likewise, think about a simple product you can offer to your customers when they purchase another product from your business website.

If your dropshipping store is selling paddle boards, you can include free board wax or maybe an ankle leash. By doing this, when the customer decides to shop for the board, he gets an additional product he didn't pay for. It's a great way to tempt customers to purchase from your business and other competitors.

Keep in mind that your potential customer will certainly compare your product offerings with those of your competitors. So, you must try to do everything you possibly can to tilt the scales in your favor. Do this only if it doesn't hurt your bottom line. If your costs increase while the earnings stay the same, you will lose more money than you earn.

Supplier Reviews

If you're shopping online, chances are you go through different customer reviews before purchasing. You might have done this on websites like Shopify, Amazon, eBay, or AliExpress. Likewise, even your customers will want to see some reviews to help make up their minds.

If you're just getting started with dropshipping, it's highly unlikely you'll have any testimonials or product reviews to place on your website. However, your customers will certainly be interested in knowing about what others have to say about the business and products you offer. It is where social proof steps into the picture.

You can increase your overall conversions by providing good reviews and customer testimonials. So, how can you do this in the initial stage? The simplest way to do this is by asking your suppliers for reviews. Don't ask all the suppliers; instead, focus only on those suppliers whose products are selling best. If you're dealing with a worthy supplier, he'll have a database of all the reviews on their website or dealer portal. So, obtaining such information and then placing it on your website can help build trust. Also, it makes your business seem more trustworthy.

Urgency and Scarcity

Nothing creates more demand, like urgency or scarcity. It is one of the reasons why online shopping places come up with different sales and offers. You might have had the first-hand experience if you've ever shopped online. For example, whenever a sale is going on, you might have noticed "Only eight items left!" or "Offers valid while supplies last!" messages while shopping. It's a simple and effective tactic to gently nudge potential customers to make a purchase.

Even you can use a similar tactic to increase the rate of conversions on your website. A simple technique you can use is a countdown timer, which is user-based. These timers automatically adjust the countdown according to the visitor. Or even a general countdown timer on the website's homepage will do the trick. For instance, if you're offering free shipping for a limited time, make certain this offer is visible on your website.

While using this technique, ensure that the offers expire. If the offer stays even after the expiration date you suggested, your website will lose credibility. Being fake will cost your business in the long run. So, be transparent, and don't try marketing gimmicks you don't intend to follow through on.

Conclusion

Once again, thank you for choosing this book. I hope you found it engaging and informative. I also hope it answered any questions you have about dropshipping. By now, I'm confident you've got all the essential information to get started on your dropshipping business.

The concept of dropshipping is relatively new when compared to other business models. But, it's one of the most lucrative e-commerce models and a great way to generate passive income.

The information in this book will not only be helpful for those who are curious to learn more about dropshipping, but also for those who want to start their own entrepreneurial venture. If you want to become a successful dropshipper, there's no time like the present to start.

Remember, choose a profitable niche and source only the best suppliers. Once you have everything in order, create your own dropshipping business and get started. Keep updated on all the different changes taking place in the world of e-commerce. Never stop learning.

Before you make any business decisions, ensure that you do plenty of research. Also, calculate your risk tolerance and never invest more than you can stand to lose. Be patient, consistent in your efforts, and put in the necessary hard work. By doing all this, your dropshipping business will be profitable. Once everything is in order, you can start earning passive income from this business.

So, what are you waiting for?

Thank you and all the best!

YOUR OPINION IS IMPORTANT TO THE AUTHOR:

If you enjoyed reading this book, and found it informative, please be kind as to leave the Author a positive and constructive review on the Amazon book page *"Write a Customer Review"* section.

Many Thanks for your support!

References

40 Brilliant-but-Easy Ways to Build Your Email List. (2018). Retrieved https://www.verticalresponse.com/blog/40-brilliant-but-easy-ways-tobuild-your-email-list/

Dropshipping Affiliate Programs - Find the Best Dropship Affiliate Program. (2019). Retrieved from https://www.dropshipstrategy.com/affiliates

Dropshipping: a Simple and Profitable Sales Funnel – Ninjaseller Blog. (2019). Retrieved from https://ninjaseller.io/blog/dropshippingprofitable-sales-funnel/

Enfroy, A. (2018). Affiliate Marketing for Ecommerce: 10 Ways to Boost Your Sales - Ecommerce Platforms. Retrieved from https://ecommerce-platforms.com/articles/affiliate-marketing-forecommerce

Ferreira, N. (2019). 16 Dropshipping Tips to Increase Leads for New Entrepreneurs - Oberlo. Retrieved from https://www.oberlo.in/blog/16-dropshipping-tips

Finding the Perfect Dropship Suppliers | SaleHoo. (2019). Retrieved from https://www.salehoo.com/dropship/finding-suppliers

Haselden, J. (2018). How to Sell on Amazon for Beginners: Step-bystep to FBA. Retrieved from https://www.nchannel.com/blog/howto-sell-on-amazon-for-beginners-using-fba/

Hassan, W. (2018). The Advantages of Creating a Sales Funnel for Your Business. Retrieved from https://menaentrepreneur.org/2018/11/the-advantages-of-creating-asales-funnel-for-your-business/

Kenton, W. (2019). Scalability: What It Is, and How It Works. Retrieved from https://www.investopedia.com/terms/s/scalability.asp

Lazazzera, R. (2019). What is Dropshipping: Dropshipping 101 for Beginners. Retrieved from https://www.abetterlemonadestand.com/what-is-drop-shipping/

Long, J. (2019). 6 Steps to Building a Successful Online dropshipping Business. Retrieved from https://www.entrepreneur.com/article/297744

Macdonald, M. (2019). How to Build an Email List that Builds Your Ecommerce Business. Retrieved from https://www.shopify.com/blog/build-email-list

Mineo, G. (2017). 55% of Visitors Spend Fewer Than 15 Seconds on Your Website. Should You Care?. Retrieved from https://blog.hubspot.com/marketing/chartbeat-website-engagementdata-nj

Shewan, D. (2019). Our 13 Best Social Media Marketing Tips EVER!. Retrieved from https://www.wordstream.com/blog/ws/2016/01/11/social-mediamarketing-tips

What is Dropshipping | How does dropshipping work?. (2019). Retrieved from https://www.shopify.in/guides/dropshipping/understandingdropshipping

Made in the USA
Las Vegas, NV
15 June 2022

50258394R00061